Cosmopolitan Islanders

Cosmopolitan Islanders is an expanded version of the Inaugural Lecture delivered by Richard J. Evans as Regius Professor of Modern History at Cambridge University in 2009. A leading historian of modern Germany himself, he asks why it is that so many prominent British historians have devoted themselves to the study of the European Continent. Books on the history of France, Germany, Italy, Russia and many other European countries, and of Europe more generally, have frequently reached the best-seller lists in Britain. They have also been translated into the languages of the countries they have been written about, and often exerted a considerable influence on the way these nations understand their own history. Yet the same is not true in reverse. On the European Continent, historians research, write and teach mainly about the history of their own country.

Cosmopolitan Islanders traces the evolution of British interest in the history of Continental Europe from the Enlightenment to the twentieth century. It discusses why so many British historians have chosen to study European history rather than work on Britain, how they learned the necessary languages, and what impact their work has had on the countries they study. British historians are still the most cosmopolitan in the world outside the USA, but the long tradition of British writing on European history is now under threat from a number of quarters, and the book ends with some reflections on what needs to be done to ensure its continuation in the future.

RICHARD J. EVANS is Regius Professor of Modern History at the University of Cambridge and a Fellow of Gonville and Caius College. A Fellow of the British Academy and the Royal Society of Literature, Professor Evans has also taught at Birkbeck, University of London, where he was Vice-Master, and the University of East Anglia, where he was Professor of European History. His books include *Death in Hamburg*, winner of the Wolfson Literary Award for History and the William H. Welch Medal of the American Association for the History of Medicine; *Rituals of Retribution*, winner of the Fraenkel Prize in Contemporary History; *In Defence of History*; and *The Coming of the Third Reich* and *The Third Reich in Power*, both History finalists in the *Los Angeles Times* Book Prizes. His latest book is *The Third Reich at War*, which completes his trilogy on Nazi Germany. He is currently writing a history of Europe in the nineteenth century.

COSMOPOLITAN ISLANDERS

British Historians and the European Continent

RICHARD J. EVANS

CAMBRIDGE
UNIVERSITY PRESS

CAMBRIDGE UNIVERSITY PRESS

Cambridge, New York, Melbourne, Madrid, Cape Town, Singapore,
São Paulo, Delhi

Cambridge University Press
The Edinburgh Building, Cambridge CB2 8RU, UK

Published in the United States of America by Cambridge University Press,
New York

www.cambridge.org
Information on this title: www.cambridge.org/9780521137249

First published 2009

Printed in the United Kingdom at the University Press, Cambridge

A catalogue record for this publication is available from the British Library

ISBN 978-0-521-19998-8 hardback
ISBN 978-0-521-13724-9 paperback

To my fellow-students

CONTENTS

FIGURES

This short book is a much-expanded version of my Inaugural Lecture as Regius Professor of Modern History in the University of Cambridge, delivered on 18 May 2009. By custom, an Inaugural Lecture by the holder of this position has sought to say something about the nature and study of history itself, and its place in the wider community, as well as speaking to the newly appointed incumbent's own particular field. I have tried to combine all these various features of the Inaugural Lecture in the present work. It addresses, and indeed celebrates, the long tradition of British scholarship on the history of the European Continent, a tradition of which I am myself a part, and it asks how this tradition has developed, why it has now reached its apogee, and what measures government bodies, schools and universities will need to take if it is going to continue. It cannot hope to match the impact of my predecessor's Inaugural Lecture, Quentin Skinner's *Liberty Before Liberalism*, any more than I can hope to attain in my field the distinction he has achieved in his own, but it does aim to make a modest contribution to the growing literature on the history of History-writing in Britain and, more generally, to the ongoing national conversation about multiculturalism, Europeanism, and British – more specifically English – national identity.

Many previous Regius Professors of Modern History have made their own, often very significant contributions to the history of the European Continent, from William Smyth, who wrote extensively on the French Revolution, through Sir John Seeley, whose first major historical publication was a large-scale biography of the Prussian reformer Baron vom Stein, and the cosmopolitan Lord Acton, who taught a Special Subject in the History Faculty on the French Revolution and whose lectures on the subject were published after his death. G. M. Trevelyan, though mainly known nowadays for his writings on English history, also published a three-volume life of the Italian nationalist and revolutionary Giuseppe Garibaldi, and J. B. Bury was the author of a history of the Papacy in the nineteenth century, while, nearer to our own day, Owen Chadwick and Patrick Collinson both wrote histories of the Reformation, Geoffrey Elton *Reformation Europe*, and Quentin Skinner *Foundations of Early Modern Political Thought*. So the tradition of writing on Continental European history in Britain embraces a good number of my predecessors as well; some of them at least are discussed later on in this book.

The book is divided into five chapters. In the first, I try to establish the basic contours of present-day British work on European history and explain why it has been so influential. I have also added to the analysis some rough-and-ready statistics about the study of foreign history in universities in France, Germany, Italy, the UK and the USA, to illustrate the extent to which the historical profession in these countries shares, or does not share, a strong and continuing interest in the history of other countries than its own (British historians' interest in Europe has always been focused on a wide variety of countries, but the largest numbers have focused their attention on France, Germany, Italy and Russia, so I have mostly followed suit and concentrated on them too). The universities surveyed were, in the United Kingdom, Birmingham, Cambridge, Glasgow, King's College London, Leeds, Nottingham, Oxford, University College London, Warwick; in France, the Université Paris-Sorbonne (Paris VI) and the Université Toulouse II (Le Mirail); in Germany the Eberhard-Karls-Universität Tübingen, Goethe-Universität Frankfurt am Main, Humboldt-Universität zu Berlin, Leibniz-Universität Hannover, Ludwig-Maximilians-Universität München, Rheinische Friedrich-Wilhelms-Universität Bonn, Ruprecht-Karls-Universität Heidelberg and Universität Potsdam; in Italy the Università di Bologna and Università di Pisa; and in the USA, Brown University, Columbia University, Duke University, Harvard University, Stanford University, the University of California at Berkeley, the University of Chicago and Yale University. The members of each History Faculty or Department were listed with specialisms, if provided, and checked against their publications. Altogether, 1,471 historians were examined: 93 French, 336 German, 92 Italian, 472 British and 478 American. Some historians study more than one country or period, so that some of the figures add up to more than 100 per cent.

Chapter 1 also draws on the responses I received from a large, though far from comprehensive, sample of more than sixty British historians who work on aspects of European history in the present day, when I wrote to them asking what impact their books had had in the countries they wrote about. The questionnaire was sent out in December 2008. Obviously the responses are subjective, indeed in some cases they are quite passionate. They articulate feelings as much as sober self-analysis; this is one reason, indeed, why many of the views they convey make such compelling reading.

The second and third chapters briefly trace the evolution of British interest in the history of Continental Europe from the Enlightenment to the twentieth century, focusing on the surprisingly large number of historians who were drawn into this subject, both well-known, such as G. M. Trevelyan, Sir John Seeley, Lord Acton or, coming closer to the present, A. J. P. Taylor, Richard Cobb and Sir Michael Howard, and less well-known. Chapter 2 takes the story roughly up to the beginning of the First World War, when European History was very much a minority interest in Britain, focusing first, for many decades, almost exclusively on the French Revolution, and later broadening out to cover Italy, Central Europe and the Balkans. The third chapter takes the story through the interwar years, when interest in the Continent was dominated by diplomatic historians who were also in many cases closely involved in government policymaking, and then charts the explosion of interest triggered by the presence of a large body of émigré historians in Britain, and the participation of a whole generation of British historians in the Second World War. These historians were able to train a younger, and very large generation of historians, the 'baby-boomers' born after 1945, in European history; this generation, my own, has produced a large body of work in the field, and is only just now beginning to reach the age of retirement.

Chapter 4 analyses the responses from living British historians of Europe to the question of how and why they decided to devote their career to France, Germany, Italy,

Russia or Spain rather than to Britain. The diversity of experience and motivation is striking, but for all the delight many of them take in emphasizing the role of chance circumstance in their decision, some common patterns are still discernible. Finally, Chapter 5 presents their accounts, again widely varying, of how they managed to learn the language or languages they needed to do their work, and discusses their views on what kind of future the study of European history faces in Britain in an age when language-learning in this country is undergoing rapid and seemingly irreversible decline. It concludes by interrogating the concept of cosmopolitanism that lies at the heart of the book, a concept that turns out to be more ambiguous than might at first sight appear.

The contribution of the community of European History specialists in this country has been far more extensive than I originally anticipated when I sent out the questionnaire. It has in a sense transformed this Inaugural Lecture, or rather the much-extended version of it presented here, from the traditional series of *ex cathedra obiter dicta* into a more collective, more democratic exercise. I am extremely grateful to all of my respondents for taking the time and trouble to write quite lengthy and considered replies to my questionnaire, and for allowing me to quote from their responses. Often their replies were packed with entertaining and revealing detail, anecdote and reflection. Many of them revised or even overturned the initial hypotheses I brought to this subject. My thanks to them all, and my apologies for not being able to include everything they said, or everyone who responded, and for not asking everyone in the field.

A few brief notes on terminology are necessary.

'European History' as it is conventionally taught in the UK does not, somewhat oddly to, for example, American eyes, include the history of Britain, and I have adhered to this convention, rather than consistently using a more cumbersome and less familiar term like 'Continental History', in this book. History with a capital H is the subject; history with a small h, the past. I have tried to keep the scholarly apparatus of the book to a minimum, so, in keeping with this book's character as an essay based on a lecture, I have dispensed with footnotes. A guide to further reading at the end of the book indicates the sources I have used, as well as pointing to some of the key works in the field.

As always, I have a number of debts to record. My colleagues in the History Faculty at Cambridge have been generous with their help and advice, and responded with unfailing courtesy to my questions. Andrew Wylie, my agent, has been supportive as usual. Richard Fisher and his team at Cambridge University Press have been encouraging and enthusiastic and done wonders with a manuscript they received only on the second day of March, 2009. Victoria Harris and Hugo Service have helped with the research, the former by generating the graphics in Chapter 1 and the latter by supplying the statistics for them, and both of them, as well as Chris Clark, Bianca Gaudenzi, Mary Laven, Pernille Røge and Astrid Swenson, read through the book at short notice at the copy-editing stage and made many useful critical suggestions. Hester Vaizey kindly read the proofs and saved me from numerous errors. The Workshop on Modern German History at Cambridge, and the graduate students taking the M.Phil. in Modern European History listened to some of my ideas at earlier stages of their gestation. Christine Corton, with our sons Matthew and Nicholas, helped keep me going during the final frantic rush of completion. I am grateful to them all. Finally, the dedication, an allusion to the invocation with which Lord Acton opened his own Inaugural Lecture more than a century ago, records my deepest debt.

Cambridge

March 2009

1

Unequal exchanges

I

In his brilliantly written and thought-provoking book *The History Men*, first published in 1983, the seventeenth-century English history specialist and regular reviewer for the *Observer* Sunday newspaper, John Kenyon, told the story of the development of the historical profession in Britain since the early modern period. He focused above all on the many British historians, especially those based in Oxford or Cambridge, who had contributed to building up the teaching and writing of History over the past few centuries, delivering sharp and acute critical judgments on a number of them as he went along. The core of History teaching and research in England was, and should be, Kenyon thought, English history, and particularly English political and constitutional history. Raising his gaze momentarily from Cambridge (from where he had himself gone into exile to Hull some years before, but where his spiritual home evidently remained), he cast a jaundiced eye across to the new universities that had been established in the 1960s and found, to his disapproval, that many of them included extra-European History on their curricula. He roundly dismissed this as faddish and ephemeral: 'hastily cobbled-up courses on Indochina or West Africa faded away as soon as these areas ceased to be of immediate current concern'. Kenyon thought that British historians had made no notable contribution to this particular field. 'Nor', he went on, 'did the contribution of British historians to European History constitute an important or influential corpus of work.' So he ignored this too.

Kenyon was not alone in this view. In his book *The English Historical Tradition since 1850*, published in 1990, Christopher Parker similarly assumed that English historians had written overwhelmingly about the history of their own country. A more recent survey, Michael Bentley's *Modernizing England's Past: English Historiography in the Age of Modernism 1870–1970* (2005), also writes as if English historians wrote exclusively about English history. On a broader front, an excellent collection of essays published under the editorship of Stefan Berger, Mark Donovan and Kevin Passmore, *Writing National Histories: Western Europe since 1800* (1999), found historians in Britain, France, Germany and Italy of interest only insofar as they wrote about the history of their own country, focusing on the ways in which they contributed to legitimizing and defending the identity of their own particular nation-state. True, there were, they pointed out, significant transnational and intercultural factors at work in the emergence of the historical profession, most notably the enormous influence exerted on historians of other countries in the nineteenth century by the research methods – lumped together under the general heading of 'source-criticism' – and the institutions – such as the research seminar – developed by German historians such as Leopold von Ranke. But when it came to examining what such historians had actually written, it was a different matter. Ranke, for example, wrote histories of England, France, the Papacy, he even wrote a history of the world, but it was his history of Germany that formed the object of attention in the essay in the collection devoted to him by Patrick Bahners.

The universality of Ranke's focus was perhaps unusual in the nineteenth century; even before his death, German historians of the 'Borussian school' were turning their gaze inwards, to the history of their own country. Yet in fact some historians have always written about countries other than their own. And nowhere is this more striking than in Britain at the beginning of the twenty-first century. British historiography spans the globe and is astonishingly broad in its coverage. Contrary to what Kenyon claimed, British historians have made a major and distinguished contribution to the History not only, understandably enough, of the British Empire but also of the many parts of the world that at one time or another belonged to it, from America to Africa, India to Australia. University courses on these areas of the world have proved both successful and durable. Specialists in these fields occupy important Chairs in many different universities.

Just as significant, however, has been the contribution of British historians to writing and teaching the history of the European Continent and the many countries it contains. A moment's thought will reveal a dozen or more prominent historians in Britain writing in the past few decades who have published major books about the modern history of Germany (Ian Kershaw, Richard Overy), Spain (Paul Preston, Raymond Carr, Helen Graham), Italy (Denis Mack Smith, Paul Ginsborg, Lucy Riall), France (Theodore Zeldin, Robert Gildea, Olwen Hufton), Russia (Geoffrey Hosking, Robert Service, Orlando Figes, Catherine Merridale), Poland

(Norman Davies), Greece (Mark Mazower), Romania (Denis Deletant), Sweden (Michael Roberts), Finland (David Kirby), Bulgaria (Richard Crampton), the Netherlands (Jonathan Israel, Simon Schama) and many others while, for many British historians of the medieval and early modern periods, writing about the European Continent is almost second nature. Books on the history of these and other European countries, and of Europe more generally, have frequently reached the best-seller lists in Britain. And these are merely the tip of a considerable iceberg, with substantial numbers of more junior historians writing on the history of various European countries, making their reputations with this work and rising up through the ranks. There are flourishing societies in Britain devoted to Continental history, each with its own academic journal – *German History* for the German History Society, *French History* for its French equivalent. Continental history is taught in the schools, notably at Advanced Level, so much so indeed that a concern is sometimes raised that the school History curriculum is focused too much on Hitler and Stalin and not enough on the past of the United Kingdom. At universities there are lectures on virtually every period of European history, and virtually every part of the Continent.

Does this reflect a broad and long-established tradition of writing on European history, or is it a more recent development? If it is relatively recent, how, when and why has it emerged? What impact have British historians had in the countries they write about? Are British historians unusual in comparison to those based in other countries in writing about countries other than their own? Edward Acton, who teaches Russian History at the University of East Anglia, sees a variety of traditions, focusing particularly on specific, cataclysmic events, such as the French and Russian Revolutions or the Third Reich. 'Strip them out', he says, '. . . and I suspect our attention would have been much weaker. Rather than seeing the tradition as reflective of central features of British society, culture and historical sense', he adds, 'I would tend to see it as always a minority pursuit, battling against the studied resistance to explicitly comparative history that so weakens Anglo-Saxon history.' Sir Ian Kershaw, whose two-volume biography of Hitler immediately established itself as the standard work when it was published in 1998–2000, agrees. He sees British historians focusing particularly on 'major episodes such as the European Reformation, the French Revolution, the Russian Revolution, the two World Wars, the rise of Nazism, the Cold War, and so on'. But, in fact, there is a good deal of evidence to suggest that this has not been the case in recent decades, when British writing on European history has covered a vast range of periods and subjects. True, there are peaks of interest in topics like the Third Reich, but one can find courses in British universities on medieval France, early modern Italy, eighteenth-century Germany and much more besides. The British interest in, and contribution to, European History is astonishingly broad.

Yet the same is not true in reverse. On the European Continent, historians of Britain, as of other foreign countries, have made little impact, apart from a handful of exceptions; there, historians research, write and teach mainly about the history of their own country. Christopher Duggan, Professor of Italian History at Reading University, thinks that 'the tradition of studying non-British countries does seem one of the remarkable strengths of British historiography (very few Italian historians, to my knowledge, work on modern non-Italian history)'. British historians have few if any rivals elsewhere in chronicling and interpreting the history of the UK. They have achieved an absolute dominance of their field that is disturbed only by the contributions of some American specialists and one or two Frenchmen, such as Élie Halévy, author of a classic multi-volume survey of English history in the nineteenth century, or François Crouzet, an economic historian who wrote significant work on British industrialization, or François Bédarida, whose social history of modern England brought new questions and approaches to bear from his background in French historical writing. French historians such as these were particularly interested in Britain when it was at the apogee of its economic and international power. They are exceptions. As Robert Anderson, who teaches European History at Edinburgh and has published widely on modern French history, especially the history of education, says: 'There is no galaxy of French historians of Britain, as there is of British and American historians of France.'

One is perhaps more likely to find influential German and Italian historians of Britain located in British History Departments, such as Frank Trentmann at Birkbeck, or Eugenio Biagini at Cambridge, than in universities in their own country. They are few in number. As Boyd Hilton, whose books, culminating in *A Mad, Bad and Dangerous People?* (2006, in the New Oxford History of England series), have transformed our understanding of politics, society and religion in England in the first half of the nineteenth century, remarks: 'With the towering exception of Halévy . . . no Continental historian has

6

had anything like as much impact on British history as (say) Raymond Carr, John Elliott, Richard Cobb, Jonathan Israel, [R. W.] Seton-Watson, Denis Mack Smith, Adrian Lyttelton, et al., et al., et al. . . . have made on the histories of their chosen countries.' Only in the History of Thought is the situation different, but thinkers such as Thomas Hobbes and John Locke are in effect universal figures whose writings attract scholars from many countries, just as do those of Niccolò Machiavelli, Immanuel Kant or Jean-Jacques Rousseau.

How can we account for this situation? Partly, thinks Leif Jerram, who teaches German History at Manchester University, this is because the study of History in a number of Continental countries is geared towards producing History teachers in the school system, whereas in the UK it has no specific purpose, but is treated as a general education that can provide a broad outlook on life and a set of transferable skills – in critical thinking, writing, debate and discussion, and much more – that will be useful in a huge variety of professions, from advertising to town planning, banking to journalism. For many decades – indeed, since the mid-Victorian era – Historical education at Oxford and Cambridge was geared, among other things, towards providing graduates who could go into the Foreign Office with knowledge of the history of other countries. 'Clearly', he concludes, 'in Britain "the world out there" has expectations of historians that go far, far beyond the formation of the nation. In France, Spain, China, Italy, "the world out there" does *not* have these expectations.'

As Director of European Exchange Programmes in Manchester University's History Department, Jerram was approached by the Universidad Autónoma of Barcelona to see if students from each university could spend a period studying at the other. The Spanish – or more precisely, Catalan – university offered survey courses, above all, on the history of Catalonia, 'highly descriptive, entirely sequential, seeing them as designed for the formation of the appropriate national citizen'. In Manchester, by contrast, the survey courses addressed a dizzying variety of topics – 'A Gendered History of the United States', 'Late Imperial China', 'European Intellectual History', 'The Cultural History of War', 'The British Empire in the Americas', 'Diasporas and Migration in the Twentieth Century', 'The History of Commodities in Latin America', 'War and Politics in the Age of Richelieu and Mazarin', 'Gender and Sexuality in Modern Africa', 'Cultures of Death and Bereavement in Victorian Britain' – 'there was no comparison', he concludes: 'Anglophone societies seem to be fundamentally as interested in the pasts of other cultures as they are in their own.'

Julian Swann, who teaches at Birkbeck, University of London, and has published books on the institutional history of *ancien régime* France, concurs: 'You can just about do a [History] degree in the UK without doing British history', he says, but 'the idea in France would be seen as absurd. Similarly, the French can't get their heads round the idea that I teach French, Italian, even Russian history, but not British; they just don't have the same possibilities.' Institutional structures in British schools and universities that divide History initially into 'British' and 'European', Swann thinks, have up to now been a major reason why 'we have turned out so many historians of Continental Europe'. It may seem faintly absurd to anyone who thinks that Britain is actually part of Europe, but it has for many decades underwritten an international breadth of approach that is lacking from the teaching of History in many other countries.

This breadth of approach has meant that many students from Continental universities have found attractive the idea of studying the history of their own country, and history on a more general, international or comparative basis, at a British university. More than one generation of European students has now enjoyed close contact with British academic life and British intellectual culture through a whole variety of exchange agreements, such as 'Erasmus' and 'Socrates', both sponsored by the European Union. EU rules oblige students from other member states to be treated on the same basis as students from the UK when they study in a British university, a further incentive to undertake an exchange or even a longer-term stay. Patrick Major, who teaches European History at Reading and before that taught it at Warwick, reports: 'I have had endless waves of German visiting students wanting to study their own history here, always with the rationale that they wanted the Anglo-Saxon perspective.' Ignorance of the language in particular prevents a similar trade in the other direction.

The sharp boundary conventionally drawn in British education between Britain and Europe starts to dissolve once one gets back to the Middle Ages. Carl Watkins, Cambridge-based author of *History and the Supernatural in Medieval England*, published in 2007, notes that 'French, German and Italian historians have, if they deal with Britain, been more concerned to consider it in a European setting rather than as a distinct area of study.' This is perhaps understandable for the Middle Ages, before the nation-state existed and when England was for long stretches of time part of a wider European political entity, whether Viking, or Norman, or Angevin, a feature of European geopolitics that only ended with the English defeat in the Hundred Years' War and was revived sporadically thereafter, most notably after the seizure of the English throne by the Dutch monarch William of Orange in 1688. Thinking about the contribution made to English medieval History by Germans, Watkins notes that German historians, notably Felix Liebermann, did, at the turn of the nineteenth and twentieth centuries, put their skills to work on producing numerous editions of English chronicles and legal texts, perhaps reflecting a widespread German view at the time that the English and Germans were part of a wider 'Anglo-Saxon' community (whether this was defined in racial terms or not was a moot point). Indeed, as another Cambridge medievalist, Rosamond McKitterick, author of a recent biography of Charlemagne, observes, many medievalists 'think that an exclusive attention to early medieval England, or even early medieval Britain, without embracing the Continent as well, is dangerously limited (as well as dull)'.

Nevertheless, it remains the case that very few non-British historians have made any notable contribution to the study of British history in the medieval period, and few, apart from Americans, to its study in the early modern and modern eras. Over the past decades, for example, the German government has invested a good deal of money and effort into the establishment of German Historical Institutes in foreign capitals such as Rome, Paris, London, Warsaw, Moscow or Washington. These act as centres of international historical exchange, facilitating collaborative and comparative work with local historians, and relocating Germans to research the history of the country in which they are based. They sponsor the publication of research in the field, and do their best to raise the profile of German historians internationally. Yet their impact in Britain at least has been limited, as Boyd Hilton notes: the most important of the publications of the German Historical Institute in London, he thinks, has been an edition of printed reports of consular envoys to Germany in the nineteenth century.

As the Institute's current Director, Andreas Gestrich, remarks:

> the problem is that present German research on British history is not as strong as British research on Germany. This is my impression. There are definitely some very good books which deserve being taken more notice of ... However, they are fairly specialized ... We have ... some very strong British historians working on topics of continental European history and very few German colleagues ... who work on British history.

'Why is this so?' he asks. His answer is surprising. Despite often being thought of as producing highly specialized research of little appeal to the general reader, German historians in fact find it very difficult to specialize in a particular area. Before qualifying for a permanent, full-time university post, they have to complete not only a doctoral dissertation but also a second, larger thesis known as a *Habilitation*. Crucially, these have to be in two different fields (to make matters worse, the second doctorate has to be accompanied by an 'inaugural lecture' in yet another area of history). Thus, Gestrich concludes that:

> German academic training, with its tendency to force young lecturers into a variety of different fields during the course of their early career, has become counter-productive as far as the gaining of expertise and academic standing in a field outside the national German history requires more continuous effort in one field. Having a doctorate and a habilitation in British history, however, would almost surely ruin your career, as there are only three academic chairs, I think, in the whole of Germany devoted to British history. The present development of serious understaffing of the departments will probably result in cementing this de-specialisation of German historians.

And if they do venture beyond the borders of Germany, these days, he adds, it is likely not to be to Britain, but further afield.

II

These impressions can be buttressed by some unsystematic yet suggestive statistics on the research interests of university History Departments in a sample of countries (see Fig. 1). Strikingly, in the UK, some 44% of historians concern themselves exclusively with foreign history, compared to 23% of French historians, 15% of German historians and 12% of Italian historians. In this respect, therefore, British historians are almost twice or even more than twice as cosmopolitan as historians in other major Western European countries.

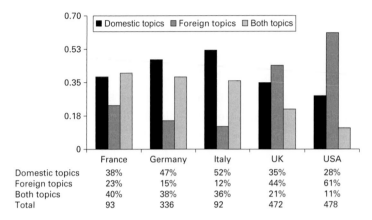

	France	Germany	Italy	UK	USA
Domestic topics	38%	47%	52%	35%	28%
Foreign topics	23%	15%	12%	44%	61%
Both topics	40%	38%	36%	21%	11%
Total	93	336	92	472	478

Figure 1. Historians working on domestic or foreign topics.

The picture is complicated, of course, by the fact that many historians study more than one country. When we turn to those who do, it becomes clear, to begin with, that comparative history is relatively weak in the UK. Thus while 40% of French historians have published on both domestic and foreign history, as have 38% of German historians, and 36% of Italian, only 21% of British historians have done so. Even more striking are the figures for the USA. The proportion of American historians who devote themselves exclusively to the study of countries other than their own is actually a majority – 61%. But comparative history is weak in the USA too; only some 11% of American historians do domestic and foreign history together. The reason here seems to be languages: British and American historians *either* study their own country's past, *or* they decide to use their command of one or more foreign languages and direct their gaze abroad; what they seldom do is both. So the dividing line between domestic and foreign history seems to be much sharper in the Anglo-American academic world than it is on the European Continent. Of all the countries studied, Italy seems to be the most inward-looking, with fully 52% of its historians devoting themselves solely to the study of Italian history; Germany comes next, with 47% working only on German history; then France, with 38% just studying French history. Once more, the proportion of historians who only look inward is lowest in the UK, with 35%, and the USA, with 28%.

If historians in all these countries look outward, to perhaps a rather surprising extent, where do they direct their gaze? The first, and most obvious, answer is that they look to the history of their own country's imperial past (see Fig. 2). Thus countries with major, far-flung and long-lasting overseas empires have a high proportion of historians who study either extra-European or a combination of both domestic and imperial history. The two most successful imperial nations in the modern world, Britain and France, each have 36% of those historians who study either foreign history, or foreign and domestic history together, engaged in research on extra-European parts of the globe.

By contrast, Italy, which only had a relatively small and short-lived empire, almost entirely located in the Mediterranean area, has 25% of historians who do not purely study Italy working on extra-European history, and Germany, whose empire was even less significant, has only 18%. Once more, however, it is the Americans who score most highly, with fully 58% of historians working on foreign history or a combination of foreign and domestic history publishing on parts of the world other than Europe: a measure, perhaps, of

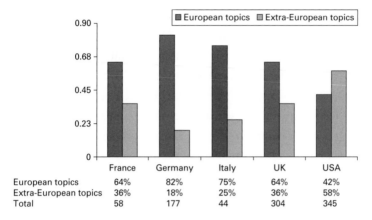

	France	Germany	Italy	UK	USA
European topics	64%	82%	75%	64%	42%
Extra-European topics	36%	18%	25%	36%	58%
Total	58	177	44	304	345

Figure 2. Non-domestic historians working on European or extra-European topics.

the current status of the USA as a truly global superpower, as well as, in a more basic sense, of its geographical location, facing both the Pacific and the Atlantic, and in close proximity to Latin America. The global reach of American historians is not matched by historians in any other country. Indeed, there is a widespread belief among the British historians whom I consulted that teaching and research on History at universities in the USA are turning increasingly away from an older-established focus on Europe, towards other parts of the world.

Nevertheless, European history is far from dead in the USA, where 42% of historians working on foreign history, either alone or in combination with domestic history, are Europeanists. Still, this is by some distance the smallest proportion of historians in any of the countries in the sample. Of British and French historians in this category, 64% concern themselves exclusively with Europe, as do 75% of Italian historians, and 82% of German historians. In this sense, therefore, a global view of history remains extremely weak in Germany and Italy. And indeed, when we put comparative historians together with domestic historians, the inward-looking nature of the historical profession in these countries becomes even clearer. Fully 88% of Italian historians write and research on Italian history either on its own or in combination with the history of another country, 85% of German historians on German history, and 78% of French historians on French. By contrast, only just over half of British historians – 56% – work on Britain, even in combination with some other part of the globe, and a mere 39% of American historians work on America.

When they do work on Europe, what countries do historians choose as their object of study? France comes out as the most popular, with 10% of German historians writing on French history, either in its own or in combination with the history of another country (including Germany itself), 11% of Italian, 10% of British, and 10% of American. Strikingly, interest in German history outside Germany itself is strongest in the UK, with 11% of historians working in this field, a reflection perhaps of the continuing central importance of the memory of the two World Wars in British culture; by contrast, only 4% of French historians work on Germany, and 3% of Italian historians. The importance not only of the World Wars but also of the Holocaust to American culture, and perhaps too the legacy of the massive German immigrant community founded in the nineteenth century, ensure that 9% of historians in the USA work on German history. In Britain, therefore, Germany is the most-studied European nation, with France coming a close second, and the proportions similar but reversed in the USA.

Italy is the third most popular nation amongst non-Italian historians after France and Germany, with 11% of French historians writing about the Italian past, 7% of German and British historians, and 3% of American historians. Of French historans, 4% research the history of Russia, as do 8% of German historians, 3% of Italian historians, 3% of British historians, and 5% of American historians. Clearly, Germany's geographical position, poised in the centre of Europe, with decades of Cold War confrontation across the border and the wall with the Communist East, has effected a lasting interest in Russian history, an interest that in some ways goes back even further, and is certainly much greater, than that evident in Britain, France or Italy.

Finally, the 'special relationship' between Britain and the USA – backed, of course, by a common language – ensures that 9% of American historians work on Britain, and the same proportion of British historians on America. Yet the mutual impact of the two historiographical traditions has been less weighty than that of, say, British historians like Sir Raymond Carr and Paul Preston on Spanish history. Boyd Hilton notes: 'There are several distinguished British historians of America, and several distinguished American historians of Britain, but I cannot think that any of them has made anything like the impact of Raymond Carr *et al.*, except perhaps for the impact of American historians on Tudor, Stuart, and earlier Hanoverian history, but then that is part of their history too.' For later periods, he describes American writing on British history, with a few exceptions, as 'respectable at best'. Interest in America amongst the historians of other European nations is much less marked, with only 4% of German historians, 3%

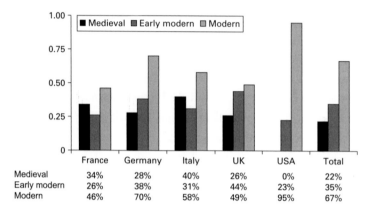

	France	Germany	Italy	UK	USA	Total
Medieval	34%	28%	40%	26%	0%	22%
Early modern	26%	38%	31%	44%	23%	35%
Modern	46%	70%	58%	49%	95%	67%

Figure 3. Historians working on domestic topics, by period.

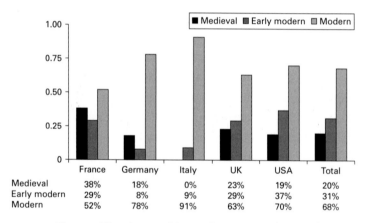

	France	Germany	Italy	UK	USA	Total
Medieval	38%	18%	0%	23%	19%	20%
Early modern	29%	8%	9%	29%	37%	31%
Modern	52%	78%	91%	63%	70%	68%

Figure 4. Historians working on foreign topics, by period.

of Italian historians and a mere 1% of French historians specializing in the field.

Amongst those historians who do look beyond the
borders of their own countries, therefore, there is a wide
variety of interest in European countries, including Britain.

18

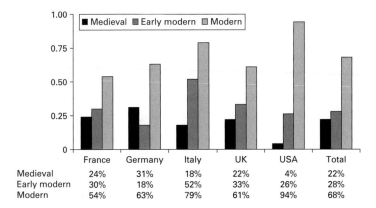

	France	Germany	Italy	UK	USA	Total
Medieval	24%	31%	18%	22%	4%	22%
Early modern	30%	18%	52%	33%	26%	28%
Modern	54%	63%	79%	61%	94%	68%

Figure 5. Historians working on combined foreign and domestic topics, by period.

Italy is by some distance the favoured object of French historical curiosity, France of the Germans and Italians, and Germany of the British (with France coming a very close second). Strikingly, a mere 7% of German historians study Britain, 4% of French and 3% of Italians, and even in the USA British history only comes joint second to France, along with Germany, with 9%. Overall, however, taking Britain, France, Germany, Italy and the USA together, excluding work on domestic history, and bearing in mind that some historians work on more than one foreign country, Germany is the most studied country, with 26% of foreign historians who work on countries other than their own publishing on its past, then Britain with 23%, the USA with 17%, France with 14%, Italy with 11%, and Russia with 5%.

If we look a little more closely at the periods studied by this sample of historians (Figs. 3–5), we can come a little closer to teasing out the nature and, by implication, the origins of their preoccupations. Those French, British and Italian historians who study only domestic history are fairly evenly balanced across the three major periods into which European historians conventionally divide their subject – medieval (before 1500), early modern (1500–1800) and modern (since 1800). However, in Germany the situation is much less balanced, reflecting no doubt the huge problems of political principle, moral judgment and national identity posed by the Nazi period: fully 70% of domestic historians study the modern period, 38% the early modern and 28% the medieval. That this is not the case with Italian historians may perhaps suggest the far smaller impact of the Fascist epoch on the national consciousness. Finally, of course, in the USA, which does not have a medieval history of its own in any conventional sense, and not much of an early modern period either, 95% of domestic historians study the modern era.

Of course, these figures do not tell the full story. History is taught and researched not just in university History Departments, but also in other subject areas as well, including Slavonic Studies, Oriental Studies, Area Studies, Modern Languages and even, in a more specialized way, Medicine and Law. Then there are separate research institutes, from the Max-Planck Institute for Educational Research in Berlin to the Institute of Historical Research in London, not to mention, as we have seen, the German Historical Institutes in a variety of countries, or the British Schools in Rome and Athens, which house not only Classicists and archaeologists, but also modern historians as well. In comparative terms, these institutional factors probably cancel each other out; it seems unlikely, for example, that there are more historians of other countries located in autonomous institutes in Germany than there are in Britain, or more in Departments of Modern Languages or Oriental Studies in France than there are in the United States. In any case, what matters in the end is what is researched and taught in university History Departments: what kind of education students get in History, how broad or narrow it is in terms of its geographical coverage. And here, British historians seem to be a good deal more cosmopolitan than their counterparts on the European Continent.

III

The differences do not stop there. Even more remarkable, perhaps, is the fact that British historians' books on European history have frequently been translated into the languages of the countries they cover, have sold well there, and have frequently exerted a considerable influence on the way those countries think about their own past. The same has in general not been true in reverse. Explaining this inequality of impact is not at first sight very easy. Boyd Hilton notes, for example, that while Halévy became interested in Victorian Britain because it was the most powerful country in the world, this was no longer really the case after the First World War, and even less after the Second, which is when the historical profession in every European country expanded at its fastest. By this time, the history of most European countries had become far more turbulent, and thrown up many more urgent questions to answer, than that of the United Kingdom. So, as Hilton concludes, 'it is hardly surprising that we have looked at them whereas they have not looked at us'. Yet, plausible though such an argument is, it still leaves many questions unanswered. British historians certainly do write and research a lot more on European history than Europeans on British, but why have they been so frequently translated, and why have they had such a marked impact on the countries they write about? The answers to these questions are inevitably complicated by wide variations in the culture and historiography of different European countries.

Take Germany, for example. 'Walk around the history section of a good German bookshop', writes Christopher Clark, who teaches Modern European History at Cambridge, and 'you still find plenty of British historians in translation'. Translation is the key. Patrick Major, Professor of History at the University of Reading and a specialist in German history since 1945, notes that 'one cannot assume that all senior German scholars automatically read the English-language literature'. But many British historians' books and articles are translated. The frequency of translation of British historical works into European languages is all the more remarkable since it is undertaken on an entirely commercial basis. The German government had for a long time provided subsidies through the Inter Nationes organization for translating German books into other languages, the French government has done the same thing through the Office du Livre, and the Italian government provides a similar service too. But there is no equivalent source of translation subsidies in Britain. Foreign publishers have to pay translation costs themselves and recoup their outlay through sales. Despite this disparity in the financial resources available, very few foreign-language history books are translated into English. Most that get across the language barrier are short textbooks on aspects of the history of the country they were written in. And even those that do make it into English are seldom very successful. Many of the potential readers for specialized works amongst university teachers and researchers have already read them in the original language, while textbooks translated from French, German or Italian are often not widely used because they are written in the context of the specific structures and demands of the educational system in their native land, not of the educational system in Britain. As Richard Fisher, of Cambridge University Press, confesses: 'Some of the least successful books we at CUP have ever published have been translations, often of "classic" works from a national historiographical tradition (e.g. Agulhon, *La République au village*). Translating specialized historical work from the language of the country being discussed is an almost guaranteed way to burn money, as no new scholarly audience is being created.'

However widespread the knowledge of English amongst the potential readership of history books, translation remains essential if a historian is to exercise any real influence in the country he or she works on. Alison Rowlands, who teaches at Essex University and has written widely on witchcraft in early modern Germany, notes: 'I find that my work is received very well as long as I give and publish papers in German.' If your major book has not been translated, as hers on witchcraft in early modern Rothenburg has not, then there are still plenty of opportunities through academic networking, where groups of researchers with common interests get together to discuss their work: German academic networks at this level have few inhibitions about including non-Germans so long as they can contribute in German and their work fits in with general pre-vailing research paradigms. 'My ideas have really had an impact in German witchcraft [history] circles', notes Rowlands, 'since I became involved in two German witchcraft research net-works, their conferences and publications. I would', she adds, 'love my book to appear in German but there seems to be little or no interest amongst publishers to pay for work to be trans-lated and I don't have the time to do this myself.' The fact is that publishers will only pay for translations of books that they think are commercially viable, and relatively specialized local studies of early modern witchcraft, however good they are, are not perceived as falling into this category.

'Germans', notes Elizabeth Harvey, Professor of Modern History at Nottingham University and author of two important books on Germany in the Nazi era, 'are very receptive to work written on Germany by British historians (and by those based in North America) and see us as part of their wider research community – while not necessarily particularly offering a "British perspective".' To be accepted as part of this research community, British historians have to speak to their German colleagues in terms they understand. Perhaps the best-known British historian working on modern Germany is Sir Ian Kershaw, whose Hitler biography received wide acclaim in German translation. 'It was marvellous for me', he writes, 'that my biography of the central figure in the central episode of German history met with such an extremely positive critical response. I have said more than once that I could not imagine a German biographer of Churchill being so warmly received here!' This positive reception may have a lot to do with the fact that he received his training in the field of

Modern German History as part of the group of social historians gathered around the Institute for Contemporary History in Munich in the 1970s by the late Martin Broszat; indeed, his first major works on Nazism appeared in German before they were published in English. His approach, in other words, is at least as much 'German' as it is 'English', and fitted in well with the trends apparent in German historical research from the 1970s onwards.

This was also, of course, a period of reorientation in German historical memory, as a new generation of Germans took a much more critical and open view of the Nazi past than their parents had done. Earlier British scholars like Alan (later Lord) Bullock, the first serious biographer of Hitler, or Hugh Trevor-Roper (later Lord Dacre), author of *The Last Days of Hitler*, were still relatively isolated figures in their own day, immediately after the war. As Kershaw remarks:

> Since the 1960s, when the break with earlier historiography prompted a positive opening towards the outside world of scholarship . . . there has been a historically motivated aversion to insularity in historical writing and readiness to accept and profit from work done abroad. Of course, Bullock, Trevor-Roper and one or two others had already made a mark in Germany, but I think it took the break with conservative historiography to instigate a significant acceleration of foreign influence on German historical writing (as long as the subject was German history!). The major spur was, I'm sure, the determination to understand how Nazism had been possible and – since the experience of the Third Reich had been world-wide – to profit from the writing of émigrés and others.

The history of National Socialism impinged very significantly on other European countries, not least on Britain, and so it is not surprising that so many British historians have taken an interest in it.

If Sir Ian Kershaw's biography of Hitler has been very warmly received in Germany, a comparable success has been achieved by *Iron Kingdom*, the history of Prussia written by Christopher Clark, which sold 80,000 copies within a year of its publication in German and secured its author a personal interview with the Federal President as well as a special feature in the country's leading news magazine *Der Spiegel*. Musing on the reasons for his book's unexpected success, Clark thinks:

> The timing was extremely fortunate: there had been no major study of Prussia for twenty years or so, and the larger political context, especially reunification, had created a new groundswell of interest in the subject, driven in part, I think, by the need to create a history that could be meaningful for east and west Germans. (This need is still not met by the academic institutions – there is no Chair of Prussian History anywhere in the former heartland of the Prussian state). Then there was the declining vehemence of the partisan battles (with their attendant methodological quarrels) that had divided German historiography since the 1960s; this created a space in which a new interpretation was not just possible but even permissible.

The reasons for the book's startling success included not only the fact that it appeared on the sixtieth anniversary of Prussia's formal abolition by the Allied Occupying Powers in 1947, the tremendous verve, flair and panache with which it was written, and the deft character-sketches it included of the Prussian monarchs and other important figures, but also its balanced and even-handed treatment of Prussia's long history, up to this point the subject either of dubious nostalgia by conservatives, or of rabid polemics by the left. *Iron Kingdom* carried out a kind of 'normalization' of a large chunk of German history just at a time, in the early twenty-first century, when there was a wide longing for it among large sections of the German reading public. As the German saying goes, Clark 'ran in through an open door'.

If one runs deliberately counter to prevailing historiographical trends, however, as Clark's Cambridge colleague Tim Blanning has done throughout his career, then one encounters some resistance, or is even ignored. His work is no less brilliant and original, but it has met with a very different reception. Tim Blanning's early monographs, arguing that the French Revolution had very little positive effect on Germany, were published at a time when German historians were trying to recover the democratic traditions they thought it had inaugurated. They were not translated. His subsequent work arguing that foreign policy had its own, independent and often determining effect on domestic events was published at a time when German historians were downgrading the importance of foreign policy and emphasizing the primacy of domestic political and social factors in Germany's relations with other parts of Europe. It was not translated either. His work on high culture and its role in the political process met with a friendlier reception, perhaps because it was directed at a less politically sensitive area and covered a broadly

European, rather than a simply German, canvas. Reflecting these various influences, *The Culture of Power and the Power of Culture* remains the only one of his many books to have appeared in German.

The factors that condition the receptivity of the German historical community to books on Germany penned by foreign historians include not only historiographical and political trends but also institutional structures. For a long time, for instance, Church history was researched and taught mainly in Theological Faculties at German universities. When Christopher Clark's first book, on German Protestant attempts to convert German Jews to Christianity since the eighteenth century through a specially established missionary centre, was published, it met with bafflement from those German historians who took any notice of it. 'The subject', he says, 'made no sense to historians trained in Germany, because it seemed to them to belong to "Church History", a musty, marginal discipline in which they had no interest . . . The UK was in this respect a far better context for this work, because everyone understood intuitively what was interesting about the questions raised by that subject matter.'

Leaping across artificial institutional barriers has its risks; but it can also provide opportunities. When I was researching my own doctoral dissertation, on the feminist movement in Imperial Germany and the Weimar Republic, in the 1970s, having chosen it as a guide to the strength or otherwise of liberal values in the decades before the triumph of Nazism, I ran into almost complete incomprehension from the archivists and historians I met in Germany (Claus Stukenbrock, the archivist who looked after me in Hamburg and who guided my subsequent trawls through the Hamburg State Archives over the following decades, was an honourable exception). I was a man, ran one frequent comment, so why was I doing this at all? More peculiar still, I was a British man, so what was I doing researching German history anyway? This view was particularly forcefully put to me by archivists in Communist East Germany, where I was informed tartly that I would do better to research the crimes of British or American imperialism. Yet in Britain, the work of liberal historians like Brian Harrison, and the emerging feminism that was so important to the History Workshop movement, made my choice seem natural enough. Later on, as a new German feminist movement emerged in the second half of the 1970s, my work was initially welcomed with a great deal of generosity, only to be subjected to heavy criticism as the movement became more radical. I became something of a bogeyman to feminist historians in Germany, because my analysis of the movement in the early twentieth century had not been entirely uncritical. Only in the 1990s did some kind of balanced reception return; but the book I wrote on the basis of my researches has never appeared in German, all the same.

I had better luck with my next two research projects. The history of medicine had been for many decades confined to Medical Faculties in German universities, where it was largely devoted to chronicling the 'march of science' in unrestrainedly positive terms. However, the rise of social history in Germany was generating a broader approach to the topic at the time, in the mid-1980s, when I published my book on the Hamburg cholera epidemic of 1892, and it was quickly translated into German, where it met with a positive reception and sold remarkably well (especially in Hamburg). Similarly with my next research book, a history of capital punishment in Germany from the sixteenth century to its abolition in East Germany in 1987. The history of crime and punishment had been studied mainly in Law Faculties, and in extremely narrow terms but, here again, social and cultural history were moving into the territory, and the book, though very long, also quickly found a German translator, subsidized by a foundation devoted to the study of violence and torture in the modern world. In both cases, in a completely unforeseen way, contemporary events had an impact, helping each book to reach a readership beyond the academic community: when *Death in Hamburg*, with its focus on state policy and public attitudes towards infectious disease, appeared, the AIDS epidemic was spreading rapidly and generating widespread public debate, while in 2001, as my book on capital punishment was being published in Germany, the Oklahoma bomber Timothy McVeigh was being executed amid a blaze of media publicity. German popular hostility to the death penalty, greater than in almost any other European country, ensured that there was a good deal of interest in the execution, helped by McVeigh's campaign to get his execution broadcast live on prime-time television. One cannot plan for such things, of course, any more than Christopher Clark could foresee the impact of his *Iron Kingdom* on Germany's historical consciousness a few years later. Chance factors also play their part in a book's reception.

German History is, perhaps more than most, riven by fierce debates that frequently find their way into the quality press, and when British historians contribute to them, they often make an impact, even if only to arouse criticism and opposition. A major intellectual influence on British historians of my generation was the New Left, and specifically the British Marxist historians – Christopher Hill, Eric Hobsbawm, Edward Thompson, Raphael Samuel, Rodney Hilton and others. Their most important and innovative work was published only after they had broken free from the shackles of Communist orthodoxy after the Soviet invasion of Hungary in 1956. Their attack on the bourgeois complacency of the Whig interpretation of history was hugely influential – far more so, I think, than the muddled and confused critique of Herbert Butterfield or the painstakingly precise, but ultimately Freud-inspired, scholarship of Lewis Namier. During the 1960s the idea of Britain as a backward country where the bourgeois revolution had never really been carried to its logical conclusion was widespread; it was put in starkly theoretical terms by writers like Perry Anderson in the *New Left Review*, and in a modified form, expressed as the need for a modernization of British institutions, it had become the dominant mantra of the Labour governments led by Harold Wilson from 1964 to 1970.

To anyone versed in this literature, it was startling to find that the left-liberal German historians of the 1970s, such as Hans-Ulrich Wehler, Heinrich August Winkler, Volker Berghahn or Fritz Fischer and his pupils, held up Britain as the modern, liberal-democratic norm from which Germany, to disastrous effect, had deviated in the course of the nineteenth and the first half of the twentieth centuries. Young British historians, notably David Blackbourn and Geoff Eley, thus mounted a full-scale assault on this view of Germany as

backward compared to Britain, generating a major controversy in the German historical profession in the process. The
controversy flared because Eley and Blackbourn spoke a language that German historians understood, and used concepts
– mostly derived from Marxist theory – that fitted in with the
terms in which the debate was being conducted at the time.

IV

It is in the end the openness of German publishers
and book-buyers to contributions from British historians
that is the most remarkable feature of the German historical scene. Similar things can be said of Italy, too. Although
Italian historians, more than most, devote themselves exclusively to the history of their own country, this national
introspectiveness has some paradoxical effects on attitudes
towards interventions from foreigners. The Italian reception of British historians' work on the Italian past has not
always been wholly positive. 'A feature of recent historiography of fascism . . . is that native historians tend to search
for the meaning of their own national fascisms exclusively
in their national pasts, while the synthesizers, the comparative historians, more open to the idea of a generic fascism,
are the "outsiders", like myself', says Philip Morgan, who
teaches Contemporary European History at the University
of Hull. Such attempts to transcend national debates on the
Fascist past have been regarded 'not exactly with fear and
loathing', he says, but at least with 'a certain wariness and
distancing'. At the same time, however, they have not been
ignored. Similarly, the Manchester-based historian David

Laven, who has published a balanced and judicious account of Venice during the period when it was part of the Habsburg Monarchy, reports that he has been widely regarded in Italy as an apologist for Habsburg rule because he does not condemn it out of hand. While liberal and left-wing Italian historians, 'almost uniformly apologists for unification', have either studiously ignored or attacked his work, it has found favour with a congeries of groups on the margins of Italian politics, such as Venetian traditionalists and South Tyrolese separatists ('none of whom', he says 'I would immediately consider natural bedfellows'). Italian historians, he thinks, prefer to hear foreigners comment on the Italian past from a distance, and he has evidently touched a raw nerve.

More distant periods are perhaps safer in this respect. His sister Mary Laven's book *Virgins of Venice* has been translated into Italian and is widely used in teaching in Italian universities. 'However', she adds regretfully, 'I don't feel that I have really cracked in to the Italian historical community, and have, alas, never been invited to one of those conferences lavishly funded by an Italian bank which should be a prime perk of life as an *italianista*.' Closer to the present day, the two books of Robert Mallett, who teaches at Birmingham University, *The Italian Navy and Fascist Expansionism, 1935–40* (1998), and *Mussolini and the Origins of the Second World War, 1933–40* (2003), 'upset many within Italian society', he says, 'who shared similar views to [Renzo] De Felice', the dominant figure in Italian historical writing about Mussolini, who had argued that the Fascist regime was not particularly close to Nazism or intent on international aggression. As a result, Mallett's work was 'initially received with some shock and controversy in Italian society' and 'repeatedly attacked in the mainstream Italian press'. Crucially, however, it presented new documentary evidence from a variety of previously inaccessible archives, and therefore, he thinks, despite the controversy, it has won a measure of acceptance within Italy. Once more, even if a British historian's work aroused an allergic reaction, it none the less made an impact.

Lucy Riall, Professor of History at Birkbeck, University of London, has also experienced some hostile reactions in Italy to her recent book on Garibaldi, which argued that he was not the simple, heroic figure of legend, but was very closely involved in the making of his own heroic myth. As 'a foreign woman exposing the myth of the only fully successful modern Italian hero', she confesses, she 'did offend nationalist sensibilities in some quarters'. However, the fact remains that these reactions came to the Italian translation of the book, and indeed all Lucy Riall's books have appeared in Italian. She puts this down in part to the fact that 'there is a long tradition of foreigners writing on Italy, and Italians in general have always welcomed this', adding that there may well be a higher percentage of translated books published in Italy than anywhere else in Europe, as well as frequent conferences and publications on the work of foreign historians in Italy. 'Almost from the beginning', she says, 'my work was greeted with interest and often enthusiasm.' In a similar way, although John Pollard, a Cambridge-based historian who writes on the history of the modern Papacy, came up against some resistance in Italy ('Italian historians, especially ecclesiastics, are rather suspicious and dismissive of the idea of the Brits working on the Papacy'), he has in general been 'treated with respect', two of his books on the Papacy have been translated into Italian, he is regularly invited to conferences, and he has a wide network of Italian colleagues and friends.

In general, in fact, as Riall notes, Italian publishers and academics have been quite open to contributions from outside. All of Christopher Duggan's books, for instance, have been translated into Italian, and the Italian edition of his recent history of modern Italy, *The Force of Destiny*, was the subject of an hour-long debate broadcast on state television's main current affairs and culture programme. He puts this down to a long-standing interest, going back over a century or more among Italian publishers and the Italian reading public, in translating and reading foreign authors. Among British historians of modern Italy, Denis Mack Smith is unquestionably the most popular. His books on Garibaldi and Cavour, Mussolini, and modern Italian history in general, have sold in hundreds of thousands in Italian translation. His success, thinks Christopher Duggan, reflects a particular aspect of British historical writing about Italy:

> his highly critical approach, especially towards Italy's
> leaders, touches a strong chord with most Italians of
> the centre and left (on the right there is a good deal of
> nationalist indignation at foreign criticism); and the fact
> that such criticism comes from Britain, whose relationship
> with Italy is for the most part historically 'untainted'
> (except, of course, during the fascist period – which is one
> reason why the far right in general takes very unkindly to
> British historians), probably helps to make it acceptable/
> welcome.

Indeed, the high status of British historical writing in Italy has been reflected in the fact that Italian universities in the 1980s and 1990s appointed a string of British historians to senior posts, including Stuart Woolf, Paul Ginsborg, Paul Corner, David Ellwood and Adrian Lyttelton.

This phenomenon has not really been paralleled in other countries and reflected at the time a process of appointment peculiar to Italian higher education, known as *chiamata diretta*: someone with a strong international reputation could simply be offered a Chair by a vote of the university faculty. Elsewhere, there is the usual process of application, subjected not infrequently to factional infighting between supporters of one candidate or another, and the machinations of powerful academic patronage networks in which outsiders are unlikely to feature. As always, of course, there are exceptions: the Scottish historian Chris Harvie, for instance, taught for many years at the University of Tübingen, and one of the editors of History Workshop, Logie Barrow, at the University of Bremen, but these were in English and American Language and Literature Departments, not in mainstream History Faculties. Such cases are rare indeed. The Italians do seem more keen on appointing foreigners to academic posts in their own universities than their counterparts do elsewhere on the Continent.

V

Openness of any kind to foreign contributions to their own history has long been much less common amongst French historians. Sometimes a British historian can have an impact by approaching history in a way that the French are ready to take up but have not yet got around to. For much of the postwar era, for example, French historians working on the seventeenth and eighteenth centuries had little time for politics and institutions, preferring, under the influence of the school of historians grouped around the journal *Annales: Économies, Sociétés, Civilisations*, founded in the 1920s by Marc Bloch and Lucien Febvre, to work on social, economic and cultural history instead. 'When I started research', recalls Julian Swann, who teaches European History at Birkbeck, University of London, and has published two books on eighteenth-century French political institutions, 'the French thought I was mad to work on the *parlements* and later the Provincial Estates, but in the last 15 years that has been transformed.'

Together with other British historians working in the same area, he has frequently been told by young French colleagues that he 'made it possible and respectable to study politics and institutions again'. The reward has been frequent invitations to conferences, examinations of theses, research centres and the like, in France. Yet at the same time, there were already signs in the 1980s that French historians were rediscovering the political, and even the *Annales* altered its subtitle in recognition of this trend. Thus Swann, though initially unfashionable, proved in the end to be swimming with the French tide. In the twenty-first century, he notes, French academia has become more interested in international co-operation; yet when he attended a large conference in Rennes in 2008, he was the only non-French participant amongst more than 200. 'French academics', he notes, 'have poor English and will put references to Anglophone works in the bibliography, but rarely engage with them. That is why I prefer now to publish more in French and go to their conferences rather than the States.'

As Robert Tombs, who teaches Modern French History at Cambridge, notes, 'foreign historians in France can often tackle topics that natives leave alone'. His own PhD was published in France ('I've just been asked to let it be republished as a "classic" – oh dear, age creeps on'). Nevertheless, he feels that French culture is not very open to outside influences, at least not compared to British. The British tradition of doing historical research on a foreign country reflects in his view, among other things,

> greater freedom to choose research topics (universities less 'feudal'); less politicization of history; the wider curricula in British universities creating jobs (I believe there is not a single chair of British history in any French history department); the greater openness and mobility within Anglophone universities (compared with France, where you are not likely to get a proper job unless you are French, educated in France, and teach French history).

This situation also impinges on the willingness of French publishers to have the work of British historians translated.

Thus Robert Gildea, Professor of Modern History at Oxford, whose work touches on more recent history and more politically sensitive topics than those of Early Modern History specialists like Swann, notes:

> My work has been well received in Britain and the US, but has had virtually no impact in France. I think there are two reasons for this: (a) I don't tell them what they want

to hear about their national myths, the Resistance etc. –
in *Marianne in Chains* I tell the story of the Academy of
Tours' refusal to publish a paper I gave to them in 1998;
and (b) a sort of closed-shop of French historians (who
also control history series in the publishing houses), who
do not want to know what non-French historians think,
or think that only French historians understand French
history. I have been invited to review in French journals,
to sit on doctoral juries, and even been given an honour
by the French government, but none of my books has
been translated into French.

Similarly, the work of the Cardiff-based historian Kevin
Passmore on French fascism has not been translated and,
indeed, he says, received very negative reviews from the
faction of French historians who opposed his interpretation.

Even when they have concerned remoter periods, the
French have seldom seen any need to translate history books
from English into their own language, since in their view, and
with relatively few exceptions, they cover their own history
perfectly well themselves. Without translation into French,
British historians cannot hope to exert any real influence. 'In
my experience', writes Peter Jones of Birmingham University,
scarcely any of whose work on the French Revolution and
the peasantry has been translated, 'it is only in the last ten
years or so that France has begun to "open up" to outside
(i.e. Anglo-Saxon) influences. Few French scholars in fields
close or identical to mine', he adds, 'are comfortable in
English, whether as a spoken or a written language.' They
are only put at their ease, says Peter Campbell, who teaches
eighteenth-century French History at Sussex, by, as they often

say, somewhat condescendingly, *'enfin un historien étranger qui parle français'*. His own books have been translated into Italian and Portuguese, but not French (though a very belated French edition of one of his books is now in preparation). French libraries often do not trouble to order copies of English-language history books, he says – and he had to donate a copy of his own to the Sorbonne – and 'British books are so expensive compared to French that no French academic would dream of ordering one.'

Yet there are indications that this situation is changing. True, admits William Doyle, who taught French History at Bristol for many years, 'it took a long time for my stuff to achieve recognition in France … I think most foreign historians of France find this.' One book was translated, in 1988, eight years after its appearance in English, thanks to the intervention of an influential French colleague, but his book on venality (the sale of government and civil service positions under the Old Regime) 'has only had a limited impact. I even', he says, 'tried to distil it by writing a *Que sais-je?* volume, but that sold so badly that they pulped most of the edition.' His best-selling *Oxford History of the French Revolution* has found no French publisher willing to undertake a translation. 'But nowadays', he continues, more optimistically, 'one gets invited to review in French, and talk at conferences, and examine theses and habilitations, so something must be getting through.' Moreover, he adds, 'over the last generation, far more historians in France have begun to recognise the importance of what anglophones do, and most of them read English easily, not to say eagerly. It's been a great cultural revolution.' Guy Rowlands, who teaches European History at the University of St Andrews, is equally optimistic. His book on the previously neglected topic of Louis XIV's army has, he said, 'had a big impact in France, though within academic circles ... French academics are much more receptive to foreign-language scholarship than they were 20 years ago.' By approaching his topic in a new and (for the French) unexpected way, he was able to make an impact. There is indeed, as Peter Campbell puts it, 'a whole new generation of young professors who speak English, are keen to make international friends ... and who see eye-to-eye on interpretations'. Networking is crucial here, too; at conferences you can meet influential review editors, heads of department and research seminar organizers, and the more historians you know in the country you are working on, the more invitations to write and speak are likely to come your way – always, of course, provided that you are up to doing it in the native language.

VI

The impact of British historians on the Continent has been complicated in some countries by the relatively long duration of dictatorships and authoritarian regimes of one kind and another. Following his victory in the brutal Spanish Civil War in 1939, for instance, General Francisco Franco held on to dictatorial power for more than three decades, until his death in the mid-1970s. The experience of British historians of Spain has been marked by both the conditions imposed by the dictatorship and the nature of the rapid transition to a modern democracy after its collapse. Thus the Cambridge medievalist Peter Linehan's first book, on *The*

Spanish Church and the Papacy in the Thirteenth Century, published in English in 1971, when General Franco was still in power, had little impact in Spain partly, he says, because of its 'lacklustre, rather nunnish title' and 'the inability of Spanish scholars to understand English'. When it was, shortly afterwards, published in a Spanish edition, its impact was further blunted by 'the coincidence of its Spanish translation with Franco's death and the general recoil from anything ecclesiastical (it was only then that the principal Spanish "authority" on the subject, a *franquista* bishop of the old school, who had praised the original to the skies without being able to read a word of it, was enabled to denounce it as "dangerous to faith and morals")'. Subsequently, however, a number of his books were translated into Spanish; from the outset, he differed from most Spanish historians in using a wide variety of archives and in dealing with the peninsula as a whole, and this undoubtedly helped their reception.

Similarly, Sir John Elliott, Regius Professor of Modern History Emeritus at Oxford, began work on Spanish history during the Franco era, and focusing on a relatively uncontroversial era; he would undoubtedly have encountered many more difficulties had he tried to research on the twentieth century. He considers himself

> fortunate in that relatively few foreigners were working on Spanish history in the post-Civil War era, and that native Spanish historians generally lacked both the resources and the time for extensive archival work. I therefore had the field very much to myself, and, moreover, was working on the seventeenth century, a relatively neglected area of Spanish history. The narrowness and bias of the official

historiography of the Franco regime meant that my textbook, *Imperial Spain*, intended primarily for an Anglo-
American readership, was rapidly taken up by Spanish
university professors looking for a more modern, and in
some respects subversive, historiographical approach,
and as a result became a standard text for generations of
Spanish students.

All his books have been translated into Spanish, and he has
received numerous honours from the Spanish crown, Spanish
governments and Spanish universities.

The experience of both historians reflects the fact that
– as Helen Graham, a leading specialist on the history of the
Spanish Civil War who teaches at Royal Holloway, University
of London, notes – for a long time, up to the mid-1970s:

> British (and to some extent also North American)
> historians were producing real, objective history, while
> inside Spain for many decades the Franco dictatorship
> only allowed the production of pro-regime propaganda,
> dictatorship masquerading as 'history'. Obviously the
> Anglo-Americans were hindered considerably by being
> cut off from contemporary archive material within Spain.
> But the very nature of Republican diaspora (including
> primary documents) to some extent remedied that, as too
> did the availability of plentiful other sources – given the
> international nature of the Civil War. Since the mid-1980s
> of course, the balance has been shifting back to Spain.

Not surprisingly, Helen Graham's books have also been
translated into Spanish, and at least one of them has sold
well among a general readership. She is following here in
the footsteps of Paul Preston, whose books have been hugely

influential in Spain. His histories of the Spanish Civil War, his biographies of Franco and of King Juan Carlos, and, above all, perhaps, his *Comrades! Portraits from the Spanish Civil War*, published in 1999, have been major best-sellers in Spanish translation, and established themselves as standard works.

VII

If British historians of Spain were first hampered by the longevity of the Franco regime, and then benefited from its collapse following the dictator's death, then British historians of Eastern Europe were in a similar situation because of the persistence of the 'Iron Curtain' until the end of the 1980s. Historical research and publication in Russia, Poland, East Germany, Romania, Bulgaria and other countries in the Communist bloc were carefully controlled by the state, which allowed only orthodox Communist interpretations to be advanced, dictated what topics should be studied, and suppressed alternative points of view when they were circulated in underground *samizdat* literature. It is here, however, that British historians gained their entry. Under Mikhail Gorbachev in the second half of the 1980s, the relaxation of controls that went under the names of *glasnost'* or 'openness', and *perestroika*, or 'restructuring', began to bring British historians' work out of this underground milieu. Almost all British historians of Russia old enough to have begun their career during the Cold War report that their work was read and discussed to some extent by dissenting and oppositional historians before 1991, and has been more widely and more positively received since then, at least during the 1990s.

Thus for example Geoffrey Hosking's 'main books have been translated into Russian and have sold quite well, especially the *History of the Soviet Union* (1985), which', he says, 'was lucky enough to coincide with *glasnost*'. One older Russian friend (born 1918) commented to me that it was the first time she had read the true story of her life.' However, Hosking's books have not, he concedes, aroused much debate in Russia, perhaps 'because my conclusions tend to be moderate and nuanced, which does not attract attention in a society where intellectuals gravitate towards the extremes. I'm currently waging a battle with the translator of my latest book, who tries to radicalize my assertions, and omits words like "probably" and "usually".'

Robert Service, author of a three-volume political life of Lenin and numerous other books on twentieth-century Russia, contrasts the relatively tolerant reception of his work under Communism with that of older Western historians and political scientists, like Leonard Schapiro and Richard Pipes, whose advocacy of the theory of totalitarianism (roughly, equating Soviet Communism with German Nazism) made them incorrigible Cold War warriors in Russian eyes. 'The Soviets', he writes,

> even before 1985, were occasionally respectful since
> my work was thought to have moved discussions away
> from the highly politicized accounts of Schapiro and
> Pipes. Reviews appeared in sections of journals devoted
> to the exposure of 'bourgeois falsification' where Soviet
> reformer-historians huddled. People like myself were said
> to be writing 'objective history', albeit history hostile to
> the Kremlin. Under *perestroika* the warmth grew. A 1988

Pravda article noted that no Soviet historian was even attempting a Lenin biography, whereas a London scholar was starting up a serious trilogy. I was also given a page to debate Lenin in *Moscow News*.

But of course it was only after the fall of Communism that Robert Service's one-volume biography of Lenin was translated into Russian. It has, he reports, been selling well, not least because it asks questions and applies analytical categories that Russian historians themselves haven't got round to dealing with yet. 'Post-Soviet historiography in Russia itself', he says, 'is still hooked on asking old questions, even if it answers them differently.'

Miriam Dobson, who teaches Russian History at the University of Sheffield and works on post-Stalinist society in the Soviet Union, concurs with this assessment. She thinks that 'there is still quite a difference ... between Russian and Western European / American approaches to history writing'. The fact that for seventy years historical research and writing in Russia were placed rigorously in the service of Communist ideology, checked, controlled, manipulated and in many cases suppressed, created a real sense of liberation when Communism finally collapsed in 1990, but what it liberated was in the first place a search for facts which for many years had been deliberately concealed from view. Much Russian historical writing has thus had a strongly empirical bent, overlain more recently by quantitative approaches, another aspect of the search for certainty and finality in historical research. 'Russian historians', she says, 'are perhaps more likely to create models to explain the phenomena they identify in their

research than we are in the UK/US.' The 'cultural' or 'linguistic turn' taken by so many historians in the West, with its
emphasis on subjectivity and uncertainty, has had little appeal
in a culture still seeking for objectivity in its representations of
the past. 'Recent debate on Soviet history in Western Europe
and the US', she notes, 'has centred on questions about the
nature of Soviet identity: did people adopt the mentalities and
beliefs nurtured by the regime? Did they "speak Bolshevik"
(maybe even "think Bolshevik"), or did citizens try to "resist
the system"? These concepts reflect our own debates about
identity and subjectivity as much as our interest in the Soviet
past, and so have had less impact in Russia.'

Such approaches can sometimes still get Western
historians into trouble, particularly when they touch on a raw
historical nerve in the patriotic climate that governs official
approaches to history in Russia today. Catherine Merridale,
who teaches Russian History at Queen Mary, University of
London, has received death threats from Russia as a result
of her book *Ivan's War*, which gives an unvarnished, though
to my mind sympathetic, account of how soldiers of the Red
Army behaved in the Second World War. Her earlier book,
Night of Stone, on suffering and death in twentieth-century
Russia, has been suppressed, she reports; in Vladimir Putin's
Russia, only positive and patriotic accounts of the past are
allowed. Nevertheless, she has been able to carry out extensive
oral history projects in Russia without too much difficulty, as
have other Western historians. Crucially, perhaps, as David
Moon, an expert on the history of the peasantry in nineteenth-
century Russia who teaches at Durham University, notes, it
has become much easier to build up personal contacts with

Russian historians since the fall of Communism. He publishes regularly in Russian-language journals and has spoken at a variety of seminars and conferences in Russia. 'Some Russian scholars', he says, 'are very generous with their time and support for foreign scholars working on Russian history.'

Despite this, the current Russian government seems intent on suppressing references to the negative aspects of the Russian past. Writing in the *Guardian* newspaper on 4 March 2009, Orlando Figes, Professor of History at Birkbeck, University of London, reported that a Russian translation of his book *The Whisperers: Private Life in Stalin's Russia*, published in the UK in 2008, had just been cancelled. The book analyses thousands of interviews, letters and diaries that give a grim picture of conditions of life under the dictatorship. On 4 December 2008, he reported, a group of masked men from the Russian General Prosecutor's office raided the St Petersburg archive run by 'Memorial', a human rights organization, where a large amount of the material collected for the book was stored, and confiscated it. Figes noted:

> At a conference in June 2007, Vladimir Putin called on Russia's schoolteachers to portray the Stalin period in a more positive light . . . Textbooks dwelling on the Great Terror and the Gulag have been censored; historians attacked as 'anti-patriotic' for highlighting Stalin's crimes. The administration has its own textbook, *The Modern History of Russia, 1945–2006: A Teacher's Handbook*. According to one of its authors, Pavel Danilin, its aim is to present Russian history 'not as a depressing sequence of misfortunes and mistakes but as something to instill pride in one's country. This is precisely how teachers must teach

history and not smear the Motherland with mud.' Danilin is . . . the editor of *The Russian Journal* . . . A special issue on the 'politics of memory' was published to coincide with the raid on Memorial. It contained two articles viciously attacking Memorial for playing into the hands of foreign historians accused of setting out to blacken Soviet history by focusing on Stalin's crimes.

Danilin, he notes, is a presidential adviser and his views closely reflect those of the current Russian leadership. Clearly, the period during which British and other foreign historians were able to have an impact on Russians' views of their own past is now coming to an end.

A rather different story is told by Norman Davies, whose two-volume history of Poland, *God's Playground*, published in 1981, and one-volume essay on Polish history, *Heart of Europe*, which followed it three years later, immediately won a reputation amongst the fiercely nationalistic Poles as authoritative and sympathetic accounts of their past at a time when Communism was still dictating officially sanctioned approaches to the past in the country. Before 1989, he reports, none of his books could be published on the eastern side of the Iron Curtain:

Copies of the English-language editions were confiscated by the police and the customs, and people were punished for possessing or importing them. One woman served a jail sentence for trying to prepare an unauthorized translation . . . Many of my writings were published underground in the *samizdat*; my name was known from broadcasts by the BBC and Radio Free Europe; and my ideas were familiar to a small circle of specialist historians

> . . . After 1989, very limited success turned to near-
> celebrity overnight. I had the good fortune to find that my
> books had been translated and prepared for publication as
> soon as the censorship collapsed. I owe a great deal to my
> Polish publishers, Znak, who had secretly commissioned
> a translation of my history of Poland in the mid-80s in
> anticipation of the political changes. As a result, *God's
> Playground* reached a hungry market almost instantly,
> before any rivals could begin to compete.

Since the fall of Communism, Norman Davies's books have all been number one best-sellers in Polish translation, while *God's Playground* was adopted as an official textbook in secondary schools. In the Ukraine, a translation of his *Europe: A History* was voted Book of the Millennium in 1999. He has received numerous honorary degrees and awards in Poland, and has become something of a national treasure.

On the whole, France aside, what is striking is the generosity with which British historians have been treated by the historical profession in the European countries about which they write. Globalization and the inexorable spread of English as the international language mean in many cases that younger historians are more open to international contacts and debates than their older colleagues. Tim Cole, who teaches at Bristol University and is the author of a study of the ghettoization of the Jews in German-dominated wartime Hungary, *Holocaust City*, reports that he is 'still seen very much as an outsider', encountering 'some resistance from older colleagues in Hungary who see me trespassing on their turf, but a more welcome response from younger colleagues who see themselves as part of a more international community and not just Hungarian history'. In the transition to a post-Communist society that has now been in progress for two whole decades, it is often difficult for older historians to break out of their previous relative isolation, while their younger colleagues are correspondingly eager to reconnect with the wider world of historical scholarship. But the same generational difference can also be seen in countries that have not experienced Communist rule, notably France; it seems in fact to be a general trend.

VIII

The unequal exchange between British and Continental historical writing and publication is clearly conditioned, then, by at least some factors peculiar to particular national cultures. But there are also some general features that deepen the overall contrast between British historians and their European counterparts. To begin with, as Norman Davies remarks, there is 'the unsurpassed British tradition of writing History as a branch of high literature'. Educated at Magdalen College, Oxford, he believes that 'my exposure at a tender age to an Oxford College with a lineage of historians running from Edward Gibbon to A. J. P. Taylor has undoubtedly made itself felt'. Similarly, Geoffrey Hosking thinks that 'where British scholars excel is the combination of sound scholarship with broad readability'. This is perhaps less of an advantage 'when it comes to scholarship for a scholarly audience of colleagues'. Nevertheless, the literary quality and broad appeal of the best British historical writing is widely recognized on the Continent. Italian publishers sell, and the

Italian reading public buys, works on Italian history by British authors, as Christopher Duggan reports, because of, among other things, 'the belief, generally well founded, that British historiography is more accessible than Italian'.

He adds that 'to a greater degree than in this country, the idea of being "popular" is abhorrent to most Italian historians, whose prose is often very dense and intended for a limited audience of specialists'. Of course there are exceptions, notably Carlo Ginzburg, whose work on late medieval and early modern witchcraft was quickly translated into English and sold well enough to go into paperback and run through several reprints. But, on the whole, Italian historical writing is closely linked to philosophy and ideology and eschews the more empirical, narrative and biographical orientations of British historiography, leaving these areas wide open to contributions from British historians. In France, historians such as Fernand Braudel, Jacques Le Goff or Emmanuel Le Roy Ladurie have written with great literary style and been translated into English. Le Roy Ladurie's *Montaillou* was a bestseller in France. But these are, on the whole, exceptions. In a similar way, Helen Graham notes that much of the work of British historians 'is written with the intelligent general reader in mind, whereas until recently that essayist tradition, writing accessibly for the public, but (hopefully) without compromising the intellectual integrity of the content, has been absent from the output of most of (even the best) Spanish academic historians writing about Spain'. Thus, where Spanish historians were failing to appeal to the Spanish reading public, British historians like (Lord) Hugh Thomas, Sir Raymond Carr, Sir John Elliott, Paul Preston and Helen Graham were able, along with American historians like Stanley Payne or Gabriel Jackson, to step in and fill the gap. Chris Ealham, who taught Spanish History at the University of Lancaster for many years, concurs. 'Spaniards', he says, 'still admire what they perceive as Anglo-Saxon powers of synthesis – this is easy to see when Spanish PhD's often run to three volumes.'

This reputation is perhaps most marked of all in Germany. As Christopher Clark notes, 'British historians still have the reputation in Germany that they actually know how to write – the sneer that used to accompany this observation has largely vanished. That', he adds, 'is surely a vindication of our essay-based approach to learning.' Startling support for this view was provided on 1 March 2007 by Volker Ullrich, Editor of the 'Political Book' review pages of *Die Zeit*, the leading cultural and intellectual weekly newspaper in Germany. 'Why', he asked, 'do the best books on Prussian-German history come from England? The answer is as banal as it is correct: because British historians write better!' Ullrich damned German historians as humourless, afraid of anecdotes, and allergic to irony and other literary devices. 'Solid knowledge of the sources and the literature, methodological awareness, clearly outlined questions – all of this', declared Ullrich, 'belongs to the historian's toolkit. But that does not make great historical writing. This emerges in the first place through the art of presentation.' In 1959, he recalled, Golo Mann, son of the novelist Thomas Mann, published a history of modern Germany that became an instant best-seller. 'A bit of narrative skill', Mann noted drily, 'and one is already an exception.' The same, Ullrich lamented, still seems to be true today. 'Because British historians think in the first place of the public and not of fellow-historians wrinkling their brows in highly specialized contemplation, they also have fewer scruples about daring to undertake a survey of a whole epoch or a major biography – the two jewels in the crown of historical writing. Is it a coincidence', he asks, 'that the most important Hitler biography has been written by a Briton, Ian Kershaw?' Or that another Briton, Christopher Clark, has written the most successful history of Prussia?

But there are also more general influences at work that make it easier for British historians' books on Germany to be translated into German than the other way round. In Germany the requirement that all dissertations should be published has generated a large, subsidized academic publishing industry, while in Britain the lack of any such requirement means that publication subsidies are virtually unknown and almost all academic publishing, even by university presses, has to be commercially viable. To put it more simply, in Germany the historian pays the publisher, in Britain the publisher pays the historian. This creates a demand in Britain for readable history books that will sell to the book-buying public as well as to students and libraries. The long German tradition of historical scholarship as a science, eschewing popular appeal, has no real parallel in Britain, where literary models of historical writing have been far more important. The difference begins already with undergraduate training, which in Britain is based on the essay, in Germany on the academic report. The result of these combined influences is that German historians have no incentive to write for anyone apart from each other and a captive readership of students taking their courses, and strive to make their reputations with the longest books, the longest sentences and the longest footnotes; British publishers look at their work with horror as unreadable and unmarketable, and seldom translate it unless it deals with a perennially popular subject such as the Third Reich.

Yet, as I have myself recently experienced, things can be equally difficult if one tries to move in the other direction with anything other than a scholarly monograph or a short textbook. A major German publisher was persuaded to buy the translation rights to a history of Nazi Germany I wrote for a broad readership in Britain and the USA, but took fright when he saw the first draft. 'You must add a thirty-page theoretical and methodological introduction', he told me, 'otherwise our readers will not take it seriously.' Loath to introduce a difference between the English and German editions, I duly wrote such an introduction for both, only to see it dismissed by English reviewers as 'pompous', 'pretentious' and 'unnecessary'. In Germany, the book did not sell well.

In general, however, British historians are not only widely perceived on the Continent as writing better, they are also seen – along with other outsiders, notably Americans – as being more objective, because they are removed from the political and other quarrels and disputes of the countries they write about. Italian historians, for example, notes Christopher Duggan, are in general closely linked to political parties and so perceived as partisan, giving rise to a 'view, at least among general readers, that foreign historians are somehow more "impartial"'. Similarly in Germany, as Christopher Clark notes: 'a foreigner can be seen as providing a more objective view from the outside (in marked contrast to Britain, where it is inconceivable that a German writing on the history of

Britain would be taken so seriously)'. In France too, says Robert Tombs, history is highly politicized, and so if you come from outside, 'you are regarded as somehow outside the domestic quarrels, and perhaps a bit eccentric. If you live long enough you become a national treasure and are given medals by the government (who tend to assume your work is a tribute to the greatness of France).' This happened in particular to the Oxford historian Theodore Zeldin, whose brilliant, six-volume *History of French Passions* became a best-seller in French translation and led to his being listed in the *Magazine Littéraire* as one of the hundred most important thinkers in the world today.

This combination of literary skill and perceived objectivity has led to many works by British historians being published in a whole variety of European languages. Obviously, a book on French history by a British historian is most likely to be published in France, a book on Italian history in Italy, and so on, but there are some topics that arouse an interest transcending national boundaries. Nazi Germany, for example, exerts an almost universal appeal because its murderous racism stands as a warning to the whole of humanity, and, within Europe, of course, because its conquests during the Second World War left scarcely a single nation untouched. My own three-volume history of the Third Reich has been, or is being, translated into Czech, Dutch, French, German, Greek, Italian, Latvian, Polish, Portuguese, Romanian, Russian and Spanish. Sir Ian Kershaw's two-volume biography of Hitler has appeared in many more European languages than this. The same broad European appeal is exerted by a variety of other topics that cross national boundaries. Thus Rosamond

McKitterick's work on Charlemagne and his age has appeared in Dutch, French, German, Italian, Polish and Spanish and has met with a favourable reception despite – or perhaps because of – its iconoclasm, a quality that has to be taken seriously because of her obvious and extremely thorough command of a vast range of sources in a variety of languages and hands.

Part of the appeal of British historians to Continental readers may lie in what Robert Evans, Regius Professor of History at Oxford and an authority on the early modern Habsburg Monarchy, has called 'the export of empiricism' and 'individualism', though, in recent decades at least, his claim that British historians have been 'largely untroubled by the presuppositions of practitioners in the target-country about their own history' no longer really holds good; on the contrary, most of them have bounced their own ideas off against such presuppositions in a highly conscious way. It remains true, however, that 'European horizons', as Evans argues, 'were as a rule loosely associated with liberal positions, rather than conservative or socialist enterprises, or with any strident political agenda on the home front.' At the same time, he notes, 'domestic concerns could give rise to benefits when they stimulated fresh exploration of other people's pasts and the application to them of new kinds of conceptual grid'.

The cosmopolitanism of British historians, then, allied to their literary skill and their reputation for objectivity (or perhaps their status as outsiders), has given them a high reputation on the European Continent and ensured the translation of many of their works into European languages, always on condition that they approach the past in a way that their potential Continental readers understand, and have the connections to smooth the path to the translation of their work. British historians are markedly more outward-looking than many of their European counterparts. In this, they resemble their colleagues in America more than historians on the European Continent. All this, however, raises some interesting and, at first sight, rather difficult questions. Where does this British interest in European history come from? Is it a recent development, perhaps? It seems on the face of it unlikely to be a product of Britain's membership of the EU, since this has always been rather grudging and half-hearted, and in any case membership of the EU has not produced any comparable phenomenon in France, Germany or Italy, despite the fact that they have enjoyed it since the beginning. Is it, then, a tradition of longer standing? And if so, how far back does it reach, and how has it changed over the years? In order to answer this question, it is necessary to go back to the Enlightenment and the subsequent development of distinctive national historical cultures and consciousnesses during the Romantic era, when the historical profession first took on its modern form.

2

The view across the Channel

I

How far back does the interest of British historians in the European past go? And what forms has it taken over the years? Answering this question is bound up with the general development of the historical profession in Britain itself. There have always been historians in the British Isles, stretching back at least as far as the Venerable Bede (672/3–735). But the teaching of History as a separate discipline is a relatively recent development. For a long time, the study of history was fundamentally a branch, first, of Christian ethics, then of literature and philosophy. True, Chairs of History were founded at Glasgow University in 1692, at Edinburgh in 1719 and at St Andrews in 1737, and the Regius Chairs of Modern History at Oxford and Cambridge were established by King George I in 1724. But there were no examinations in History, no syllabus in History, and no Faculties of History, nor were there to be any at British universities until the 1870s. Most students took pass degrees, involving a mixture of subjects, and avoided specializing in any one of them. Although the Regius Chairs had been founded mainly to give lectures that would prepare young men for government service, their status as royal appointments, and their handsome salaries, soon made them into government sinecures, to be handed out by the Prime Minister of the day in return for favours, or to cement political alliances. The Regius Professors thus did little in practice to foster the study of the subject for which they were nominally responsible. Most of them were utterly undistinguished, and some of them did not even go near the universities where they were supposed to be based.

Oxford and Cambridge dons had at the time, of course, to be Anglican clergymen. Their interest in matters academic was minimal. To the serious student, of whom there were admittedly very few, the English universities had little to offer. Famously, when Edward Gibbon (1737–94) came up to Magdalen College, Oxford, in 1751, aged only fourteen, and already a voracious reader, he was grievously disappointed in what he found. 'I spent fourteen months at Magdalen College [he wrote]; they proved the fourteen months the most idle and unprofitable of my whole life.' Gibbon fell into bad company and ran up large debts, but this was quite normal for the undergraduates of the day, and it was not until, at the age of sixteen, he announced his conversion to Roman Catholicism to his father, who, scandalized, passed the information on to his college, that Gibbon finally attracted the attention of his tutors. Since he had reached the age at which students were required to subscribe to the 39 Articles of Faith of the Church of England, it was no longer possible for him to continue. His father pulled him out of the university and sent him to study with a strictly Calvinist pastor in Lausanne. Gibbon never ceased thereafter to inveigh, when the opportunity arose, against what he memorably called 'the monks of Magdalen, steeped in port and prejudice'.

His four and a half years in Lausanne gave him a systematic education, and when he returned to England he was fluent in French, had a good command of Latin, and was reasonably competent in Ancient Greek. Gibbon assured his family after several months that he had now become a sound Protestant, but the truth was rather different: his reading had encompassed not only the Classics, but also the works of the French Enlightenment, and these had turned him into a religious sceptic and a champion of reason against faith, detachment against emotion.

Gibbon's attachment to the Classics was far from unusual. All educated gentlemen in the eighteenth century knew them; Latin and Ancient Greek formed the standard core of secondary and higher education at the time. Common familiarity with the great Greek and Roman authors transcended state boundaries in the Enlightenment, and provided models of oratory and political style in assemblies as different as the English Parliament and the French Revolutionary National Assembly. Gibbon's knowledge of the works of the French Enlightenment, and his sovereign command over the French language, in which he wrote his first publications, testified to his intellectual abilities, but they too were nothing very unusual: French was the common vernacular of the European elites; Frederick the Great of Prussia, notoriously, commented that he spoke to the members of his court in French, and reserved German for addressing his dogs and his servants. French was also the common language of diplomacy in Europe well into the twentieth century. Not to know it was not to be civilized.

An intimate knowledge of the works of Voltaire and Montesquieu was confined perhaps to serious intellectuals like Gibbon or the Scottish historians and philosophers

Robertson and Hume, but all educated men had at least heard of them, and knew a bit about their ideas. Gibbon had taken perhaps a rather unusual route to the Continent, but many others went as well, and, in particular, the so-called 'Grand Tour' was considered a virtually essential part of the education of the young English or Scottish gentleman at this time. One after another, well-off families sent their sons on a lengthy tour, lasting as much as five years, through France and northern Italy to Rome, where they were meant to drink at the fountainhead of Classical civilization, then back via Switzerland or, for the more adventurous, Germany. Gibbon too went on the Grand Tour and it was here that he found his true vocation. In his own, much-quoted words, 'It was at Rome, on the 15th of October, 1764, as I sat musing amidst the ruins of the Capitol, while the barefooted friars were singing vespers in the Temple of Jupiter, that the idea of writing the decline and fall of the city first started to my mind.' He began the project in 1770; the first volume appeared in 1776, and the final one was completed in 1787.

In his vast work, which covered the entire history of the Roman Empire up to the fall of Byzantium in 1453, Gibbon surveyed at one point or another the whole of Europe. Yet what he was writing, though it reflected an idea of a common European civilization based on the shared values of the Classical world, cannot really be called European history; there was, in essence, no concept of Europe behind it. The credit for the invention of European History in its modern form must go instead to the Scotsman William Robertson (1721–93), whose book *The History of the Reign of the Emperor Charles V*, published in 1769, took as its theme the emergence of a modern, secular, cosmopolitan Europe in the sixteenth century. Writing the book was a deliberate bid for commercial success following his earlier *History of Scotland* (1759), and Robertson, a clergyman of distinctly secular inclinations, sold his book to a publisher for an advance that quickly gained the status of legend. Like Gibbon, Robertson was interested in the contrast between barbarism and civilization, and in the state of civil society. He saw the sixteenth century as the era in which the 'great family' of European nations emerged. In this way, he both put a modern concept of Europe on the map and introduced the idea of different, successive periods in European history. Like Gibbon, he wrote a generalizing, analysing, philosophical form of history, but his gaze at Europe was for the first time directed towards the modern world rather than the Ancient.

Robertson's vision of Europe, however, was soon shattered by the cataclysmic event that above all others was to drive British concern with modern European history in the first half of the nineteenth century: the French Revolution, which undermined the assumptions both of Gibbon and of Robertson about progress and civilization. The French Revolution decisively ruptured the connections between Britain and the European Continent that had underpinned both Gibbon's vision of a universal Classical civilization and Robertson's idea of the European 'family of nations', a family of which the Scottish historian naturally assumed Britain was a member. From this point onwards, British historians saw a huge gulf between their own country and the European Continent. Of course, the idea that Britain was different from, say, France or Germany, was common enough before

1789. But what the French Revolution did was to anchor in British culture, and therefore also amongst British historians, the idea that the history of the Continent was fundamentally alien to the experience of the British Isles. In forging a specifically British national consciousness and identity, the French Revolution and the subsequent long series of wars with France, and, at times, much of the rest of the Continent, culminating in the Battle of Waterloo in 1815, created in 'Europe' for the first time a definable *other*, which invited British historians to investigate its past as if they were investigating the past of some strange and remote foreign land.

II

Gibbon's view of humanity was essentially unhistorical. He saw it as unchanging, the human mind the repository of permanent and enduring forces of reason and unreason, so that in his Roman Senators it is easy in retrospect to imagine bewigged eighteenth-century gentlemen disputing in a club instead of the forum; often, indeed, his protagonists are not people at all, but abstractions, virtues and vices of various kinds that found their expression in the behaviour of the various Emperors. Human qualities, he thought, were more obvious and more starkly exhibited in Ancient Rome than in his own time, but in essence they had remained the same. Now, suddenly, the past began to seem very different from the present, in the hands of both those who rejected it, like the Revolutionaries, and those who wished to recover or preserve it in the face of radical change. The French Revolution, as Peter Fritzsche has remarked, disrupted Western conceptions of historical continuity. It suddenly made the past different, unfamiliar, and hence more difficult to understand. And it demanded explanation in itself.

The French Revolution changed everything, including the way in which historians wrote and the subjects to which they devoted their attention. For the historians of the post-Revolutionary decades, writing under the impact of the novels of Sir Walter Scott, the Middle Ages were a period not, as Gibbon and Robertson saw them, of ignorance and decay, but of high adventure, nobility and piety. English historians continued for a time to focus on the Ancient World and, for example, a multi-volume *History of Greece* by Gibbon's friend, the Tory MP William Mitford (1744–1827), was published in several volumes between 1784 and 1810. The *History* was extremely popular, though its frequent diatribes against democracy, too obviously inspired by its author's hatred of the French Revolution, made it in the end too much of a tract for the times to endure. But by the end of the Napoleonic Wars the French Revolution was itself beginning to become sufficiently distant in time to be consigned to history.

Gibbon's reaction to the French Revolution was also hostile. He saw it as another barbarian invasion. His hostility was shared by other British writers and thinkers, amongst whom of course the most celebrated was Edmund Burke (1729–97). It was Burke who, more than anyone else, advocated the importance of organic historical identity and tradition as a source of political stability and continuity, a bulwark against the kind of atrocities committed by the French Revolutionaries in the name of abstract and timeless principle during the Reign of Terror in 1793–4. Change, Burke thought, was desirable, but it had to be gradual and, above all, it had to be consensual. Revolutionary upheavals brought only death and destruction. A decade and a half of almost continuous warfare against Napoleon, whom most Britons saw as the heir of the Revolution rather than its negator, only served to deepen this conviction amongst conservatives. As the Revolution receded into the past, so British historians began to apply themselves to describing its disastrous course and horrendous consequences.

At Cambridge, the Regius Professor of Modern History, William Smyth (1765–1849), who was appointed by King George III in 1807 and stayed in office for the next forty-two years, delivered a lengthy series of lectures on the French Revolution, which were eventually published in three volumes in 1840; he continued in office for another nine years until his death at the age of eighty-four. The fifty-four lectures provided a full and detailed narrative, and lost no opportunity to characterize, as he wrote, 'all the great measures of the popular leaders as ill judged or criminal', from their 'usurpation of power' from the Estates General onwards. The abolition of religion was, he declared, one of many 'frightful extravagances' committed by the Revolutionaries, and he continued, in a grand peroration:

> And it is these frightful extravagances of which the human mind was seen to be capable, these scenes of affliction and despair, the wide-wasting cruelties, the unutterable horrors, by which these new opinions were accompanied, that must henceforth teach their own lesson: they must show the value of every writing, usage and institution, that can have any tendency to keep

men within the paths of sobriety and duty; keep them aware of the imperfections of their nature, submissive to the dispensations and conscious of the presence of their Almighty Judge. These are the lessons, and this the permanent benefit, which, it is to be trusted, mankind will hereafter receive from this most appalling portion of the history of Europe.

As for the cause of the Revolution, Smyth put much of it down to the French love of fashion. 'A cry for the States General became the fashion; they were therefore to be called. The Revolution was the fashion; there was, therefore, to be a revolution. Anything old was out of fashion; there was a call, therefore, for everything that was new.' Such frivolous subservience to the dictates of fashion was, Smyth scarcely needed to imply, quite alien to the conservative and traditionalist cast of mind that had preserved social peace intact in Britain.

Smyth was generally regarded as a Whig of the old school, a fact indeed to which he owed his appointment as Regius, and his views were close to those of Edmund Burke. He was disenchanted with the new, reformist Whiggery of the 1830s. An admirer of Gibbon, he nevertheless grew increasingly religious and conservative with age, and regarded modern notions of progress with distrust. Other British historians of the French Revolution were similarly convinced that it demonstrated the superiority of British institutions. A four-volume history of the Revolution by Charles Macfarlane (1799–1858), published in 1844–5, made it clear that the Revolution had happened in France and not Britain because France, unlike the United Kingdom, was 'a despotically and ill governed country – quite as much from the incapacity of the people for a rational liberty, as from any superiority of their sovereigns in the arts of despotism and oppression'.

The best-selling *History of Europe from the Commencement of the French Revolution in 1789 to the Restoration of the Bourbons in 1815* by Sir Archibald Alison (1757–1839), an Edinburgh lawyer, was published in no fewer than twenty volumes between 1833 and 1842, reprinted ten times by 1860, condensed in a one-volume edition and simplified still further for use as a school textbook. It surely owed much of its success to the glow of satisfaction that must have spread over its British readers when they contemplated the contrast between France, still after 1815 groaning under what Alison called an 'Asiatic despotism', and their own fair country. The Table of Contents gives some idea of the flavour of this comparison:

> Total destruction of the old landed aristocracy . . .
> Immense subdivision of the land of France. Deterioration
> of the condition of the French people, and their
> agriculture, in consequence – Diminished morality among
> the people of France – Diminished material comforts of
> the French people . . . Astonishing successes of England
> in the war. Prodigious maritime successes of Great Britain
> during the war – Great colonial conquests of England
> during the same period – Internal growth and prosperity
> of England during the same period . . . How has this
> vast dominion arisen – First cause – the energy and
> perseverance of the British people.

Nevertheless, Alison did not intend his enormous work to engender complacency in its readers. There was an ever-present threat that England might go the same way, he warned.

The 1830s and early 1840s, when his volumes were published, were a period when industrialization, growing social antagonisms, the demand for political reform, and the emergence of radical movements such as Chartism were posing, in the eyes of Tories like Alison, a clear threat to social stability. He warned, therefore, that the gap between rich and poor had to be narrowed, and the twin threats of poverty and rising crime rates dealt with. He pointed to what he saw as the corrosive effects of the 1832 Reform Act, and warned of 'the perilous nature of the current into which men are drawn, who commit themselves to the stream of political innovation'. France, he concluded, had 'eaten of the forbidden fruit, and she is reaping the appropriate punishment'. His book therefore was a demonstration of both the benefits he thought Britain had gained by not going down this road, and the disasters that would occur if it did; Alison was also writing, after all, under the impact of the 1830 Revolution in France, which opened up once more the alarming prospect of political instability in Britain's nearest neighbour.

The French Revolution was thus the first and overwhelmingly the dominant topic of interest for those British historians who concerned themselves with the European Continent in the first half of the nineteenth century. Men like Alison and Smyth used the abundant memoir literature and published documentation to write very extensive and detailed accounts of the Revolution; the Irish-born lawyer and politician John Wilson Croker (1790–1857) amassed a large collection of pamphlets and ephemeral literature from the Revolution, with which he wrote a series of no fewer than thirty articles for the *Quarterly Review*, disinterring often minor and obscure figures from the dustbin of Revolutionary history; he has some claim to be counted as the first historian of the Revolutionary crowd. He corresponded with surviving participants in the Revolution and was far more similar to a modern researcher than either Alison or Smyth. But his obsession with detail prevented him from ever writing a general history of the subject, and he remained in many ways true to the existing British tradition of Burkean hostility; the Revolutionary crowd was for him not a crowd but a mob, suborned by unscrupulous agitators, and driving on the Revolution to madness and destruction from the very beginning.

Madness and destruction were also what a very different historian, Thomas Carlyle (1795–1881), saw in the French Revolution; but in a positive rather than a negative sense. Born in Dumfriesshire, Scotland, to parents who were both pious and poor, Carlyle studied at Edinburgh University, where he said he learned little from his instructors but managed to master a variety of foreign languages including Italian and German. His Presbyterian parents instilled in him a strongly religious cast of mind, which remained even after he had abandoned formal observance, and this doubtless was one factor that made him respond with enthusiasm to the German Romantics, whose works he began to write about in the 1820s. These ideas found expression in his essay *Signs of the Times*, published in 1829, a sharp attack on utilitarianism. By the 1830s he had moved to London and after writing the obscure mystical fantasy *Sartor Resartus* he became an overnight sensation with a three-volume history of the French Revolution, published in 1837.

Carlyle was a social and moral prophet as much as he was a historian. He detested the rationalism of the Enlightenment and sought faith instead in the transcendentalism of the German idealists, which became for him the essential substitute for the dogmatic Calvinism of his parents. The human experience of the individual was central to these beliefs, situated in the endless flux of time; and Carlyle believed that humanity was being crushed under the weight of the machine age in which he lived. In his writing therefore he sought to recover the natural force of human experience, the expression, he thought, of Divine purpose in world history. Thus History was 'the only *articulate* communication . . . which the Past can have with the Present': communication through the lives of individuals. Carlyle thought that individuals were the agents of Divine Providence, and thus of course what he called 'Heroes' were the supreme actors in history. Yet history was in the end unfathomable; God's purpose could not be discerned by men. 'Alas for our "chains", or chainlets, of "causes" and "effects"', he wrote. History had to be seen as a whole, and the historian had to 'inform and ennoble the humblest department with an Idea of the Whole'. That meant seeing the individual in the flow of time. At the same time, our knowledge of the whole could only ever be imperfect; we could only approach God's perfect revelation, which existed in eternity, through its partial revelation in time. Carlyle's technique of grasping this revelation was to transmit the 'chaos of being' in his writing, and he did so in a kind of ecstatic collage, made up of many different sources and bits of sources flung together to make as vivid an impression upon the reader as possible.

For Carlyle, there was no more dramatic example of the emergence of elemental human forces into modern history than the French Revolution. Carlyle's work *The French Revolution* is not, to put it mildly, a conventional work of history. Carlyle was writing before most primary sources were available, and he did no archival research. He relied instead on the memoirs of participants, of which there were many; he read most of them, and underneath the delirious surface of his prose, his representation of people and events was accurate enough, and often very detailed. What struck readers, however, was above all Carlyle's vivid depiction of the great events of the Revolution, the uprisings, the riots, the votes, the executions. For Carlyle, for example, the crowd that stormed the Bastille 'was a living deluge, plunging headlong . . . plunging through court and corridor; billowing uncontrollable . . . Blaze of triumph on a dark ground of terror; all outward, all inward things fallen into one general wreck of madness!' The rest of his depiction possessed a similarly rhetorical quality.

Carlyle thus went against much British writing about the Revolution up to this point, against the negative judgments of, say, William Smyth or Archibald Alison (whose multi-volume epic was appearing at the same time as Carlyle's). He was not interested in drawing contrasts with Britain, and the lessons he sought to draw were not political but moral, and so universal. Carlyle saw the French Revolution in positive terms, and he celebrated not just the constitutional reforms of its early phases, but the violence and bloodshed too, including the Terror. Not for him the complacent contrast with the virtues of British constitutionalism that underpinned the writing on France of so many of his British contemporaries.

72

As time went on, indeed, Carlyle exhibited a growing contempt for democracy, bureaucracy, in fact any other means of running the state apart from the rule of one, heroic individual, exemplified in his next major historical work, on Oliver Cromwell. This tendency came out most strongly of all in his biography of Friedrich II of Prussia, *Frederick the Great*.

Frederick the Great was not an obvious subject for Carlyle's hero-worship, though his knowledge of Germany and German history almost predestined him to turn to a German topic once he had dealt with the French Revolution:

> French Revolution having spent itself [he wrote], or
> sunk in France and elsewhere to what we see, a certain
> curiosity reawakens as to what of great or manful we can
> discover on the other side of that still troubled atmosphere
> of the Present and immediate Past . . . What part of that
> exploded Past, the ruins and dust of which still darken
> all the air, will continually gravitate back to us . . . ? Only
> what of the Past was *true* will come back to us . . . In which
> point of view, may not Friedrich, if he was a true man and
> King, justly excite some curiosity again; nay some quite
> peculiar curiosity, as the lost Crowned Reality there was
> antecedent to that general outbreak and abolition?

Carlyle admired Frederick because of his persistence and his refusal to despair in the face of seemingly overwhelming odds, but on the other hand the Prussian monarch was far from 'true'; on the contrary, he was notoriously devious and deceitful, and Carlyle was in the end forced to suppress most of his hero's deceptions rather than admit that he went against his own principles of honesty and sincerity. The biggest problem for Carlyle, however, was that Frederick lived a very long life, so that the vividness and immediacy of detail which were the most striking features of his three volumes on the short period of the French Revolution inevitably became diluted, and the project itself stretched out much further and took much longer than Carlyle originally intended. In the end it took up six volumes, published between 1858 and 1865, produced virtually simultaneously in English and German. Well before he completed the last one, Carlyle had become bored. 'The dreary task', he said at the end, 'and the sorrows and obstructions attending it . . . [are] now happily over. No sympathy could be found on earth for those horrid struggles of twelve years.'

In preparing for the book Carlyle consulted all the literature he could find. He used research assistants who obtained material for him and provided the volumes with a scholarly apparatus. And he visited Germany to see for himself as many as possible of the places in which Frederick's life was lived. The result was an almost unmanageable mass of material, which Carlyle clearly found very difficult to control. Reviewers were quick to point out that the book could have been shorter. One remarked that the first two 'enormous volumes', which appeared together, might have been cut by half 'on the easy plan of excluding all the oaths, one half of the exclamations, a third of the repetitions, and a fourth of the needless minutiae'. Another wrote later, of all six volumes:

> As to *Frederick*, it is not a book at all, but an encyclopedia of German biographies in the latter half of the eighteenth century . . . Who cares to know how big was the belly of some court chamberlain, or who were the lovers of some unendurable *Frau*? What a welter of dull garbage! . . . O,

Thomas, Thomas, what Titania has bewitched thee with
the head of Dryasdust on thy noble shoulders?

Clearly, the subject of Frederick the Great, a cold rationalist of
the Enlightenment, was in the end unsuited to Carlyle's delirious depiction of eruptions of human emotion.

Nevertheless, the biography sold well, despite the
criticisms it encountered. Notoriously, the Nazi Propaganda
Minister Joseph Goebbels was an avid reader of the book in
the last days of the Third Reich and presented Adolf Hitler
with a copy in the Berlin bunker, reading him passages that
would encourage him to believe that he could escape from
the enemies who surrounded him just as Frederick had done.
And indeed Carlyle's views were in many ways congenial to
the Nazis. Carlyle was not only obsessed with heroes and what
he termed 'Great Men', he distrusted reason and elevated
emotion, he glorified in violence and destruction, and in
some of his other, late writings he dismissed philanthropy
and humanitarianism and he poured contempt upon Jews
and Africans. In his account of the Prussian King's battles, his
treatment of his subjects, and much else, Carlyle's worship of
dictatorship and naked force comes through with disturbing
clarity.

Yet for all his idiosyncracies, and for all his unequivo-
cal damnation of many of the most widely accepted political
principles of his own time, Carlyle proved surprisingly influential on other historians. Key aspects of Carlyle's philosophy
of history struck a chord amongst many historians of the later
nineteenth and early twentieth centuries. One of the most pro-
lific of these was the Protestant Irish historian William Lecky

(1838–1903), who never held an academic post, though he was offered the Regius Chair at Oxford in 1892. He knew Carlyle and had long conversations with him on their walks together through London. In books such as *The History of Rationalism in Europe* and *The History of European Morals from Augustus to Charlemagne* he explicitly adopted Carlyle's emphasis on free will and accident in history; he saw history in terms of the interplay of will and desire, and argued that man was 'not a mere passive weed drifting helplessly upon the sea of life, and human wisdom and human folly can do and have done much to modify the condition of his being'. Only by recognizing this fact could we learn from history the mental discipline that would enable us to live a moral life in the present. Somewhat surprisingly, Lecky devoted 500 pages of his *History of England in the Eighteenth Century*, published in five volumes between 1878 and 1890, to the French Revolution, focusing on its foreign relations. Lecky condemned the Revolution for adopting 'a system of cosmopolitan politics' which 'discarded all national traditions'. Once more, a British historian (and Ireland at this time was part of Britain) saw the history of the European Continent not least in terms of providing dramatic lessons for the British present.

III

In the middle decades of the nineteenth century, British historians' interest in the French Revolution began to wane; the 1848 Revolution inspired not further apprehension, but liberal optimism, as the prospect of a more progressive and democratic France began to open up, at least for a while.

Far more important, however, was the fact that French historians, notably Taine, de Tocqueville and Sorel, were now writing major works on the Revolution of 1789, which were translated into English and so widely read that it scarcely seemed necessary for English historians to tackle the subject. Nevertheless, European History continued to be taught in the universities. Smyth's successor at Cambridge, Sir James Stephen (1789–1859), appointed on the advice of the Prince Consort when the popular historian Thomas Babington Macaulay (1800–59) turned the job down, also lectured on Modern French History until his death in 1859 at the age of seventy. These lectures were generally poorly attended, as Stephen complained; the problem was that there was as yet no Honours degree in History, so that lectures had to appeal to the vast majority of students who took a pass degree, or in other words, as Stephen was told, they had to be on British history. In any case, Stephen, a former Secretary of State for the Colonies, did not live in Cambridge, wintered abroad for health reasons, and when asked to report on his subject by a Royal Commission in 1852, replied, in a letter from Paris: 'Of the actual state of historical studies in the university I know and can report nothing.'

Stephen's successor Charles Kingsley (1819–75) was far more successful, and his lectures, also covering a variety of topics in Continental European History from 'The Invasion of the Teutonic Races' to 'The Congress of Vienna', are said to have attracted large audiences. This was not merely because of their historical content, however, or because of Kingsley's undoubted personal charisma, but also because of Kingsley's national reputation as a Christian moralist and fiction-writer. He achieved lasting fame not as a historian but as the author of a novel about a chimney-sweep, *The Water-Babies*; as a writer of historical fiction, notably *Hereward the Wake* and *Westward Ho!*; and as the proponent of what were called 'muscular Christianity' and 'Christian socialism', whose values he contrasted with the secular ideologies of the French Revolution. In his 1867 lectures on 'the *Ancien Regime*, as it existed on the Continent before the French Revolution', Kingsley relied heavily on Alexis de Tocqueville's celebrated and compelling account of the topic; but his real point was to draw lessons for the present and, once more, this pointed irresistibly to the contrast between the misery of the French and the happiness of the British. 'There exists in Britain now, as far as I can see', he proclaimed, 'no one of those evils which brought about the French Revolution' – no poverty, no discontent, no despotism, no excessive centralization of government: a view that reflected the optimism of the mid-Victorian age in which he wrote, and contrasted strongly with the anxieties expressed by Archibald Alison three decades before.

Kingsley thought that the social peace which Britain did indeed enjoy in the 1860s had deep roots in English history, particularly in the relative openness of English society. The French nobility, indeed all nobility on the Continent, had been a 'caste', quite unlike its English counterpart. The Revolution, Kingsley concluded, had brought many 'horrors', but it had been unleashed by oppression, by a lack of the liberties which the Anglo-Saxons had handed down to eighteenth-century England, and by excessive poverty. Kingsley used these conclusions to argue that the extension of voting rights under consideration in Parliament as he wrote, and eventually carried in the Reform Act of 1867, was a wise step that further cemented the bond in Britain between the rulers and their subjects, a bond sadly lacking in France under the *ancien régime*. The Revolution had, in his view – again contrasting with those of Alison and Smyth – brought liberty to wide areas of the Continent. It had thus, in the end, not been an unmitigated disaster. It had been a necessary, 'purifying fire'.

All these historians, whether or not they taught in a university, were essentially men of letters. They did not carry out original research using unpublished documents, and they did not adopt or apply the principles of scientific historical scholarship as they were being developed in Germany. But in the last quarter of the nineteenth century, the discipline of History in Britain did undergo a rapid process of professionalization. The Honours School of Modern History at Oxford was founded in 1872, and History gained its own curriculum at Cambridge with the founding of the Historical Tripos in 1873, a move which also involved the creation of the History Board. In 1875 ten students graduated in History, and throughout the 1880s the numbers were generally in double figures. They expanded steadily if unevenly from this point on. It was Sir John Seeley (1834–95), a Classical scholar appointed Regius Professor of Modern History in 1869 largely because Prime Minister Gladstone admired his (anonymously published) life of Christ, who was the moving force in the process of professionalization at Cambridge; a brilliant and popular lecturer, he broke with precedent by actually living in Cambridge, and held seminars for advanced undergraduates, an innovation that owed a good deal to the German example. Seeley dismissed Carlyle and Macaulay (whose *History of England* was probably the most admired and most popular work of history written in the nineteenth century) as 'amateurs' and regarded original research as the lifeblood of the historical profession. Indeed he condemned the Tripos examination as an irrelevance which could, as he said, 'mar the effectiveness of my teaching', and argued that examinations were not appropriate for History students at all.

Seeley's eventual fame, and his knighthood, were achieved with a large tome on the rise of the British Empire, *The Expansion of England*, published in 1883, which included the famous statement 'we seem, as it were, to have conquered and peopled half the world in a fit of absence of mind'. But he had made his reputation as a historian with *The Life and Times of Stein, or Germany and Prussia in the Napoleonic Age*, published in three stout volumes in 1878. Although Seeley's background was in Ancient History, in which he had a more than respectable publication record, his appointment as Regius Professor made him feel obliged to shift periods and write a major work on a topic of more recent vintage. Stein was, and is, something less than a household name in Britain. He was a radical reformer who took the lead in rationalizing the Prussian state after its catastrophic defeat by Napoleon at the Battles of Jena and Auerstedt in 1806. Among his measures were the emancipation of the serfs and the introduction of compulsory military service, uncoupling the structures of the Prussian military state from their previous entanglements with the system of relations between landowners and serfs. Seeley's interest in him was twofold.

First, he was writing at a time when Germany was being unified under the leadership of the Prussian statesman

Otto von Bismarck, and he wanted to give the British reading public a clear idea of how the new German Empire had originated and what values it incorporated. Politics, in Seeley's famous *dictum*, was present history, history was past politics, and the links between past and present were always present in his mind. Secondly, this was, in a slightly oblique guise, another example of the continuing British obsession with the French Revolution and Napoleon. Seeley boosted Stein's importance far beyond what was warranted, to make him into Napoleon's greatest foe, and portrayed him as the embodiment of national consciousness and nationalist enthusiasm, in contrast to Napoleon's drive to enslave the whole of Europe under his dictatorial rule. Virtuous, modest, restrained, rational, the embodiment of rational Protestant sobriety, Stein was for Seeley the antithesis of vainglorious French licentiousness.

The Life and Times of Stein was not a success. Packed with tedious detail of Stein's administrative reforms, it seemed too boring and too remote to offer any really interesting explanation of the long-term origins of Bismarck's success in the present. Seeley hugely overestimated the popular contribution to Napoleon's overthrow and, in making the contemporary parallel, he ignored what was obvious to many of his contemporaries, namely the authoritarian and undemocratic elements in Bismarck's new creation. The book had none of the epigrammatic liveliness of some of Seeley's later works, and was widely ignored. Seeley ran into a good deal of criticism for both the book's style and its substance. Why had it been so badly received?, he asked bitterly: 'It is because our insularity is really brutalizing us.' At least English readers had heard of Napoleon, so he turned to writing a biography of the first French Emperor instead of continuing his preoccupation with Germany.

For Seeley, Napoleon was an utterly cynical megalomaniac, unscrupulous and immoral; his opponents in Europe were the true champions of liberty. But this view ran into criticism – particularly, of course, from Napoleon's many admirers. Seeley turned instead to British history, and particularly to British foreign policy. His disillusion went so far as to lead him to oppose the study of European history, which, as one College supervisor remarked, he thought best left to the 'École Normale, Victoria University [of Manchester] and the inferior universities of Germany'. This was not, however, because he thought that British History should be the exclusive object of study at Cambridge, but rather because, as a believer in scientific history, he opposed broad survey papers in English as well as European History, which he described as encouraging 'the boarding-school view of history', opening up 'a vista of unending cram'. Instead, he preferred to encourage students 'to write dissertations involving original research' and infusing the study of history with the methods and principles of political science.

In Seeley's day, the Historical Tripos at Cambridge did include an element of Modern European History as well as a Special Subject on Medieval Italy. Under his successor, Lord Acton (1834–1902), three new European papers were introduced, in 1897. But then, Acton was a European through and through. The centrality of Continental Europe to Lord Acton's historical thought stemmed not least from the fact that he himself was to all intents and purposes a Continental

82

European. He was born in Naples in 1834 into a cadet branch of an English noble family that had made its modest fortune through service with the Kingdom of Naples. Their Roman Catholicism had excluded them from the English Establishment, but his grandfather had inherited the family title and estates in Shropshire when the main line died out in 1791. Using his Neapolitan court connections, Acton's father had married into the German aristocracy, and indeed Acton himself, after being educated in Paris, also married into the Bavarian family of Arco-Valley, which much later achieved notoriety when one of its members shot dead the leader of the socialist revolution in Munich at the end of the First World War, Kurt Eisner. Acton spoke French, German and Italian fluently, and spent a lot of his life in Bavaria. His Catholic connections included an uncle who was a Cardinal, and his relations with his teacher at Munich University, the liberal theologian von Döllinger, always remained close. So confused and obscure was his nationality, when nationality was not very firmly fixed anyway, that his son eventually found it necessary to establish himself as a British subject by getting a special, private Act of Parliament passed in 1911.

After the death of Acton's father in 1835, his mother remarried George Leveson-Gower, who became the second Earl Granville in 1846. A Whig aristocrat who got on well with his young stepson, Granville served in every Whig or Liberal government until his death in 1891, and provided Acton with an automatic entrée into the world of the great Whig families and leading Liberal political circles; this seemed to predestine him for a political career, and he duly entered Parliament, but he lost his seat in the Commons and Gladstone persuaded

Queen Victoria to raise him to the peerage in 1869, the first Catholic to be ennobled for over 180 years. Yet Acton was no ordinary Catholic, and he had little or no contact with the English Catholic community, which he considered backward and dogmatic. When he issued his famous *dictum* 'power tends to corrupt, and absolute power corrupts absolutely', he was in fact writing about the Popes, who had in his lifetime so disastrously, in his view, departed from the principles of liberal Catholicism to which he himself adhered. Acton was English enough to regard liberty and free thought as the central principles of political and social life, and he abhorred Pope Pius IX's issuing of the Syllabus of Errors in 1864 and his Declaration of Papal Infallibility in 1870. Acton and Döllinger fought the latter decree tooth and nail: Döllinger was excommunicated as a result, while Acton's attempt to steal incriminating documents from the Vatican Library was only foiled by an advance warning given to the French troops guarding Rome by a friend who did not want him to get into trouble. Warned of the danger that Acton might be excommunicated too, Prime Minister Gladstone declared: 'They will never excommunicate an English peer.' And they never did.

As a member of the Liberal governing elite, Acton was widely known to the most influential circles as a historian of unparalleled learning, and in 1895 a word in the right ear secured him the appointment by the Liberal Prime Minister Lord Rosebery as Regius Professor of Modern History at Cambridge. He took his duties seriously, abandoning his habitual winter quarters in Cannes for a room in Trinity and delivering lectures to packed and excited audiences of undergraduates. The following year he was asked by Cambridge

University Press to edit a new project, the *Cambridge Modern History*. Alas, it was all too late; already in his sixties at the time of his appointment, he suffered a serious stroke in 1901 and left for Tegernsee in Bavaria to convalesce; he never recovered, and died there the following year.

How did this cosmopolitan, liberal, Catholic background influence Acton's view of history? In a sense, it was surprisingly English. In his Inaugural Lecture as Regius Professor, he argued that Continental European History needed to be taught and studied in England because the unwritten, organic and almost unconscious formation of the British Constitution over the centuries failed to deliver any 'equivalent to the vivid and prolonged debates in which other communities have displayed the inmost secrets of political science to every man who can read'. For open debates on politics and the constitution, taken to first principles, it was necessary to look to the Continent, to Paris, Frankfurt or Geneva, as well as to the United States. 'The foreigner', declared Acton, 'has no mystic fabric in his government, and no *arcanum imperii*. For him the foundations have been laid bare; every motive and function of the mechanism is accounted for as distinctly as the works of a watch.'

Acton famously sought to put his vision of a neutral, objective history into effect in the *Cambridge Modern History*, but died before the series got very far beyond the planning stage. 'No compilation at second hand from the best works would meet the scientific demand for completeness and certainty', he told his contributors, so he decided that the *Cambridge Modern History* was to consist of 'original work' rather than being merely a 'serious compilation', an admirable if somewhat impractical intention that would have condemned the contributors to a similar fate to his own, of reading more and more, and always putting off the fateful day of actually writing down any conclusions.

Acton also envisaged a pan-European history rather than a country-by-country approach. He declared:

> Universal history is not the sum of all particular histories, and ought to be contemplated, first, in its distinctive essence, as Renaissance, Reformation, Religious Wars, Absolute Monarchy, Revolution &c. The several countries may or may not contribute to feed the main stream . . . [but] attention ought not to be dispersed, by putting Portugal, Transylvania, Iceland, side by side with France and Germany . . . My plan is to break through the mere juxtaposition of national histories and to take in, as far as may be, what is extra-territorial and universal.

Thus chapters were to be defined 'not by a limit of years, but by some salient point and catchword'. This would have made for an interesting, if rather uneven, set of volumes that would have revealed a lot about the conceptions and preconceptions of the Edwardian historical profession, but it was in the end not very practical. Acton's successor as General Editor, Sir Adolphus Ward (1837–1924), whose books included *The House of Austria in the Thirty Years' War* (1869) and *Great Britain and Hanover* (1899), abandoned it in favour of a largely country-by-country approach, ignored altogether the advice of Acton's Inaugural Lecture, to 'study problems not periods', and produced in rapid succession a competent and comprehensive survey of the political history of every country

86

in Europe, in twelve turgid volumes, which appeared in the short space of eight years before the First World War, and remained for decades an essential crib for undergraduates, though no sane person would ever try to read them through from start to finish.

Acton did not like the Middle Ages. He regarded modern history as beginning with the Renaissance, when Europeans reconnected with the learning of the Ancient world and began to think for themselves once more in an 'awakening of new life' that inaugurated a 'forward movement' that continued to his own day. He thought that this movement was driven on in particular by revolutions, and he rejected the argument of what he called 'the Conservative line of writers, under the name of the Romantic or Historical School, [which] had its seat in Germany [and] looked upon the [French] Revolution as an alien episode, the error of an age, a disease to be treated by the investigation of its origin', in favour of 'the Liberal School, whose home was France, [which] explained and justified the Revolution as a true development, and the ripened fruit of all history'. Acton adhered broadly to the Whig theory of history, which saw English history as a successful struggle for the liberties of the people against obscurantism and conservatism. Yet in his view the struggle fought out in the English Revolution of the seventeenth century was not won until the French Revolution of the eighteenth made its influence felt – 'another and more glorious Revolution, infinitely more definite and clear-cut, with a stronger grasp of principle, and depending less on conciliation and compromise'.

Acton's lectures on the French Revolution, delivered in the late 1890s to a Special Subject class on the topic, and reconstructed subsequently from shorthand notes, were a paean of praise to the moderate constitutionalists amongst the Revolutionaries:

> By right of the immense change they made in the world, by their energy and sincerity, their fidelity to reason and their resistance to custom, their superiority to the sordid craving for increase of national power, their idealism, and their ambition to declare the eternal law, the States-General of 1789 are the most memorable of all political assemblies.

Louis XVI, by contrast, got only bad marks from Acton. Down to the last he was complacent, 'unconscious of guilt, blind to the opportunities he had wasted and the misery he had caused'. Yet for all his praise for the constitutionalists, Acton conceded that they made the mistake of failing to provide checks on their own authority. This opened the way to the Jacobins, who aimed at a 'dictatorship', to concentrate all powers in the centre and destroy many of the liberties so recently achieved. Ruthless and well organized, they soon set in motion the Reign of Terror with its mass guillotining of the Revolution's supposed opponents.

Acton carefully charted the narrative of events down to the fall of Robespierre – 'the most hateful character in the forefront of history since Machiavelli reduced to a code the wickedness of men' – but made it clear that the Terror was mainly born of paranoia caused by the Austrian-led invasion of France. The lectures ended with the triumph of Napoleon, 'through whose genius the Revolution was to subjugate the Continent'. Acton held a strong admiration for

Napoleon ('the most entirely known as well as the ablest of historic men'), who completed the work of the Revolution. Napoleon indeed, he thought, was 'the most splendid genius that has appeared on earth'. Perhaps nowhere does Acton's Continental background play more of a role than here: for British writers, Napoleon was the arch-enemy in the long war whose culminating points had been Trafalgar and Waterloo; for Continental intellectuals, by contrast, he was the man who destroyed encrusted despotisms, swept away petty states, reformed bureaucracies, modernized laws and in general brought the benefits of the French Revolution to Germany, Italy and the Low Countries.

Acton's positive view of the French Revolution signified the degree to which he stood apart from the long tradition of English writing on the topic. By the end of the nineteenth century, the best British scholarship was devoted mainly to synthesizing the work of French historians like Alphonse Aulard, who were pioneering the archival study of the Revolution. The Scots scholar Henry Morse Stephens (1857–1919), who published a three-volume history of the Revolution in 1886–91, shortly before he left to take up professorships first at Cornell, and then at Berkeley, in an early example of the 'brain-drain', embodied a new attempt to gain an objective, even neutral perspective on the events of 1789–94, though his reliance on French work in the field gave his own history a strongly pro-Revolutionary bias, and led him even to excuse the Terror as a necessary and inevitable episode whose architects were seeking to build a 'stronger and more glorious France'.

Acton's hero-worship of Napoleon was still unusual even in the late nineteenth century. Less so perhaps was his negative judgment on Prussia and the Prussians, which derived from his central concern for the history of liberty. 'No people', he said, 'were more submissive, or more ready to suffer, for the sake of the State.' The rulers and the people in Berlin 'could not help being aggressive, and they worshipped the authority that could make them successful aggressors'. Militarism, devised by the Prussians and exported to Russia at the time of Peter the Great, posed a huge threat: 'the tremendous power, supported by millions of bayonets, which grew up . . . at Petersburg, and was developed, by much abler minds, chiefly at Berlin . . . is the greatest danger that remains to be encountered by the Anglo-Saxon race'. As a Catholic with strong south German connections, Acton disliked the Prussians, opposed Bismarck's expulsion of Austria from Germany during the unification process in the 1860s, and was horrified by the German Chancellor's attempt to suppress the independence of the German Catholic Church during the so-called *Kulturkampf.*

His cosmopolitan background made him unsympathetic to German or indeed any other kind of nationalism. He believed strongly in multicultural, multi-ethnic states such as the Habsburg Monarchy, and regarded a state based on a single ethnic group as a serious threat to liberty. The co-existence of different nations in a single state was, he argued, 'a test, as well as the best security of its freedom. It is also one of the chief instruments of civilization; and, as such, it is the natural and providential order, and indicates a state of greater advancement than the national unity which is the ideal of modern liberalism.' Nationalism, he declared, 'does not aim either at liberty or prosperity, both of which it sacrifices to the imperative necessity of making the nation the mould and measure of the state. Its course', he predicted correctly, at least as far as the twentieth century was to be concerned, 'will be marked with material as well as moral ruin.' He was also a stern critic of imperialism: 'In judging our national merits', he wrote, 'we must allow much for our national hypocrisy. Wherever we went, we were the best colonists in the world, but we exterminated the natives wherever we went. We despised conquests, but we annexed with the greed of Russia.' If there was one consistent thread in his unconventional and often paradoxical life, it was a strong distrust of power in any form.

IV

For all his distrust of Germany, or at least of Prussia, Acton was indebted to the Germans in one centrally important respect: he was a true believer in the ideal of professional History propagated by the followers of Ranke. In 1886 he gave institutional expression to this idea by taking a leading part in the foundation of the *English Historical Review*, a learned journal which he intended, along the lines already laid down by Germany's *Historische Zeitschrift*, to present the latest fruits of professional, scientific historical scholarship to its readers. Acton wrote for the first issue a lengthy and entirely positive account of German historical method, which, like many subsequent British historians, he considered mandatory for any serious professional historian to apply. The journal's first Editor was Mandell Creighton (1843–1901), a cleric whose spectacularly successful ecclesiastical career as Bishop of Peterborough and subsequently of London did not prevent him from making major contributions to historical scholarship. Creighton's programme for the *English Historical Review* was remarkable for the breadth of its ambition. It rejected, for example, the idea that it should confine itself to publishing articles on political history, declaring that its subject was 'the whole life of man in the past'. It wanted to establish nothing less than a 'universal record' of the past, and sought 'the help of eminent historians in Germany, France, Italy and the Scandinavian countries' in doing so. In explicitly seeking to cover foreign History as much as British, and Ancient History as much as Modern History, the *English Historical Review* already stood in sharp contrast to the *Historische Zeitschrift*, whose opening manifesto announced curtly that the Editors would 'devote more space to modern history than to earlier periods, and more to German than to foreign history'. The nationalist note indeed was sounded loud and clear in the German journal, which invited 'discussions which clearly illuminate the characteristic differences between German and foreign ways of writing history in our days', making it clear that the latter were markedly inferior to the former.

Creighton's openness to foreign and in particular European history, a trait he fully shared with the more overtly cosmopolitan figure of Acton, was exemplified in his own life and work. His wife was a native speaker of German, he translated a volume of Ranke, and his major work was a five-volume *History of the Papacy during the Period of the Reformation*, published between 1882 and 1894, in which, rather like William Robertson more than a century earlier, he sought to use the subject as a means of portraying 'the working of the causes which brought about the change from medieval to modern times' in Europe as a whole. One of Creighton's many enthusiasms was for Italy, whose unification in the *Risorgimento* of the 1850s and 1860s he applauded, and whose culture he admired so much that he gave his daughters names derived from Dante. His decision to write a history of early modern Europe focused on the Papacy was testimony to this enthusiasm. Creighton thus combined two particular enthusiasms of the British middle and intellectual classes in the Victorian era – an interest in German thought and history, most obvious in Carlyle and the circle around George Eliot, and a love of Italy and the Mediterranean.

Creighton's love of Italy was shared by his friend George Macaulay (G. M.) Trevelyan (1876–1962). Appointed Regius Professor at Cambridge in 1927, he was an extraordinarily successful historian whose book *English Social History*, published in 1942, sold 400,000 copies by 1949: an elegy for a lost rural world based on hierarchy and deference that clearly struck a chord in a readership numbed by the horrors and privations of war and postwar austerity. Trevelyan's work reflected his faithful adherence to the Whig interpretation of history, which indeed he personified as no-one else before or since. Its apogee had been reached in the person of his great-uncle, Thomas Babington Macaulay. The Trevelyans regarded English history as a progress towards liberty and democracy, fought for by generations of men like themselves, against the entrenched forces of conservatism, authoritarianism, hierarchy and tradition. This was indeed the famous Whig interpretation of history, according to which the English past was divided up into heroes, like Pym and Hampden, Cromwell,

Wilkes, Paine, Grey and many others, and villains, like Charles I or James II or George III. Events like the Civil War, the 1688 'Glorious Revolution' and the 1832 Reform Act were regarded above all as stepping-stones on the way to a liberal and democratic present. Complacent as this may seem, it also involved a strong dislike of unbridled authority, a distaste for imperialism and the oppression of other nations and other peoples, and a desire to see foreign policy used as an instrument of liberalism rather than naked national self-interest – although the two, of course, were not necessarily incompatible.

The Whig interpretation of history was not purely confined to the English past. On the contrary, it was a universal doctrine with universal application. The benefits of parliamentary rule and civil freedoms, English liberals believed, should and would in the fullness of time be extended to the rest of Europe and indeed the world. The denunciation of Continental atrocities and despotisms played a prominent part in English popular politics, especially at election time, from the popular outrage at the cruelties perpetrated by the King of Naples on political prisoners in the 1820s to Gladstone's crusade against the 'Bulgarian horrors' and the 'Armenian massacres' towards the end of the century. The English public took a close interest in Continental European affairs in the nineteenth century, and exiled liberal heroes of national resistance to Continental tyranny, such as the Hungarian leader Lajos Kossuth, were given a tumultuous welcome when they reached asylum in London. None was more fêted than the Italian nationalist leader Giuseppe Garibaldi on his visit to the capital in 1864. In the earliest stages of the wars of Italian unification, Garibaldi's guerrilla force of a thousand was joined by enthusiastic English volunteers, while educated English ladies sewed together the red shirts that the volunteers wore on their campaigns. English newspapers reported with breathless excitement the Thousand's every move, while poets vied with each other to find the most fitting way of turning their exploits into verse.

This enthusiasm for liberal ventures on the European Continent aroused in some an interest in the history of Continental countries, and in none more than in Trevelyan. For him, as for other English liberals, Italian unification was a success story without parallel. It laid to rest the internecine quarrelling of the Italian states, so often in the past the occasion for wider European conflicts. It established parliamentary government. It was not achieved at the expense of any other nationality, unlike its counterparts in Germany or Hungary – an important point for a liberal critic of imperialism such as Trevelyan. It had improved prosperity, justice, order and peace in the peninsula. For Trevelyan, Garibaldi was the Romantic hero incarnate: simple, straightforward, incorruptible, bold, generous, courageous, a born leader whose fight against clerical oppression and secular despotism brought about an era of progress, liberty, prosperity and peace. 'To us of other lands', Trevelyan concluded, 'and most of all to us Englishmen, Garibaldi will live as the incarnate symbol of two passions not likely soon to die out of the world, the love of country and the love of freedom, kept pure by the one thing that can tame and yet not weaken them, the tenderest humanity for all mankind.' After writing surveys of medieval and Stuart England, and a study of the poet George Meredith, therefore, Trevelyan turned his energies to writing a major study of Garibaldi and his contribution to the *Risorgimento* and the unification of Italy.

In choosing this topic, Trevelyan was strongly influenced by Carlyle's concept of the hero, which he imbibed during an intensive reading of the sage's works while he was an undergraduate at Cambridge. It was particularly the early Carlyle that he admired, with his contempt for the machine age, his hostility to the profit motive, his ability to convey 'sharp, living, memorable pictures' of the drama of the past, his imaginative grasp of the motives of historical figures, and his determination to write about social life as much as about politics and warfare. At the same time, he disapproved of Carlyle's later tendency to worship heroic despots like Frederick the Great. Trevelyan's heroes were liberal freedom-fighters. And among these it was almost inevitable that he was drawn to Garibaldi. Trevelyan's father had gone to Italy in 1867 with the aim, eventually frustrated, of enlisting with Garibaldi for his march on Rome. Like many other educated Englishmen, Trevelyan had been given a Classical education which instilled in him a particular reverence for Italy and Rome. By the 1890s, the Grand Tour had been replaced by more modern forms of tourism, but Italy and Rome were still favourite destinations, and Trevelyan visited them in 1895, and again, in the company of his father, two years later. His father told him stories of Garibaldi's ill-fated defence of the Roman Republic, and in 1904 Trevelyan was given a copy of Garibaldi's *Autobiography* as a wedding present; this seems to have been the catalyst, and he began work on the trilogy shortly afterwards. The first volume was published on the centenary of Garibaldi's birth in 1907 and the whole work was completed with the publication of the final volume in 1911.

Trevelyan, like Creighton, had succumbed to what the historian John Pemble has called *The Mediterranean Passion*, in his book of that title on Victorians and Edwardians in the South, published in 1987. The steamship and the railway opened up new possibilities of travel to Italy, where the Classical heritage combined with the lure of exoticism to draw in thousands of British tourists in the second half of the nineteenth century. However, on the whole they did not intermingle with the local population, stayed only a short time, lived in hotels, and devoted themselves to inspecting buildings and scenery rather than discovering the Italians. The historian Edward (E. A.) Freeman was not untypical of this kind of tourist: visiting Italy in the late 1870s, he was appalled at 'the gabble of English tourists' in Venice. He was not a tourist, he insisted, but a 'true traveller' and preferred instead to travel to the smaller and more remote towns on the shores of the Adriatic. Yet, as the archaeologist Arthur Evans, who later became his son-in-law, subsequently remarked, 'He can't or won't speak either German, French or Italian, and his daughters have to look after him and manage everything.' The English, as Pemble remarks, were never so insular as when they were abroad.

Trevelyan was unusual in the depth and seriousness of his engagement with Italy. Going far beyond the superficial acquaintance of the normal tourist, he learned to read Italian – not difficult for anyone with a good command of Latin – and, in pursuit of his subject, went to Italy and cycled around the peninsula, visiting all the major sites of Garibaldi's life and battles. Yet for all the closeness of his involvement, Trevelyan still took a very British perspective on Italian history. In a way, he saw Garibaldi as helping to make the Italians more like the British. The publication of his three volumes coincided with the apogee of liberal political success in pre-First-World-War Britain, a time of sweeping Liberal electoral victories and equally sweeping Liberal political reforms. No wonder they were successful. As portrayed by Trevelyan, Garibaldi set a heroic example for other liberals to emulate, and provided a stark contrast with the rise of authoritarian German power, a source of growing anxiety in the British political and intellectual elite at the time. Trevelyan continued to see the unification of Italy in almost wholly uncritical terms for decades afterwards. In 1933 he confessed: 'I worshipped Garibaldi. And after twenty-five years I worship him still.' He was not entirely uncritical of the Italian state of his own day, however. The unsuccessful Italian invasion of Ethiopia in 1896, followed by the successful conquest of Libya in 1911, had begun to raise doubts even in Trevelyan's mind. Moreover, Garibaldi seemed to lack any successors of comparable stature. In 1911 Trevelyan celebrated the fiftieth anniversary of unification with a paean of praise to the Italian state: 'Nothing is more remarkable – though to believers in nationality and ordered liberty nothing is more natural – than the stability of the Italian kingdom . . . The building is as safe as any in Europe.'

Trevelyan's involvement with Italy continued and deepened during the First World War, when he spent three and a half years as commander of a British Red Cross ambulance unit in the mountains to the north-west of Venice. Two more books followed: *Scenes from Italy's War*, recounting his experiences, and *Manin and the Italian Revolution of 1848*, another study of an Italian liberal hero. The latter was not a success. By the time it was published, in 1923, the building of Italian democracy had collapsed and Mussolini was in power. Trevelyan described Manin's brief tenure of power in a Venice liberated from Austrian control in the 1848 Revolution as 'a dictatorship based on popular confidence and affection', much as Mussolini was trying to project his own regime at the time and in the following years, but his overall view of 1848 was now much darker: not so much the prelude to the liberal triumph of Italian unification, as a disastrous defeat for Continental liberalism on a larger scale, leading to the rise of German despotism and the outbreak of the First World War. And indeed the war itself destroyed Trevelyan's youthful political optimism and turned him away from European history to the celebration of English liberties and English history which was to occupy him for the rest of his career. Unlike many members of the British governing elite, Trevelyan despised and disliked Mussolini, and deplored the violence of the Fascists. His visits to Italy became less frequent. 'Fascism was abhorrent to me', he later explained, 'because it set out to abolish the easy, kindly temperament of the Italian people that I loved.' Instead it was trying 'to drill and bully [them] into second-rate Germans'.

Trevelyan was not merely concerned with Italy and the Italians in his contemplation of the European Continent. The outbreak of the First World War forced him, like many others, to confront the problem of Germany, a problem that was already beginning to concern Lord Acton around the turn of the century. As a left-wing Liberal, Trevelyan was mildly inclined towards pacifism, and urged British neutrality in the European conflict that erupted in late July 1914. However, he radically changed his stance when the Germans invaded Belgium, and became convinced that, unless the Germans were expelled from France and Belgium, 'civilization as we know it is done for'. In backing the war effort he broke with his closest associates, including Bertrand Russell and his own brother, who all took a strongly pacifist line. He believed the Kaiser to be a greater threat to English liberty than Napoleon, of whom, in contrast to Acton, he also disapproved. Trevelyan spoke German, and had visited Germany as an undergraduate, but he disliked what he called 'the German character', especially its militaristic tendencies and 'the crassness that expects other people to be always on their side over everything, or else to be regarded as hostile'. At the same time, however, he opposed the Treaty of Versailles in 1919 as harsh and unjust towards Germany, believing that it saddled the infant Weimar Republic with a burden from which it could not free itself.

Trevelyan's interest in Italy and Germany was far from unique, though the depth of his involvement with Italy certainly had few, if any, parallels, and his passionate liberal engagement with Continental causes was old-fashioned even in the Edwardian period. Far more common was a view that History had to be neutral as well as objective, and that taking sides was unscientific and set a bad example to students. This attitude can be observed throughout the first half of the twentieth century in probably the majority of the British historians who turned to writing about the European Continent, and especially about the diplomatic relations of countries like Germany and France with Britain and the British Empire in an effort to understand the roots of the growing tensions of the years 1900–14, the First World War and its aftermath. Trevelyan, for all the thoroughness of his research, was still essentially a gentleman scholar of the old type, unafraid of passionate and lyrical commitment to a cause such as that of Italian unification. His vision of Europe was basically simple and straightforward, and differed not a great deal from that of the mainstream British historians who had written about the French Revolution earlier in the century: Europe lagged behind Britain in its political and democratic development, and anything that might help it catch up was to be applauded.

Already by the time he was writing his enthusiastic biography of Garibaldi, however, the historiographical landscape in Britain was changing almost out of all recognition. The idea of professional, scientific, and therefore neutral and objective, History was gaining the upper hand, exemplified by the famous Inaugural Lecture by J. B. Bury (1861–1927), appointed Regius Professor of Modern History in Cambridge in 1902, proposing that 'history is a science, no more and no less', a claim that Trevelyan polemicized vainly against in *Clio: A Muse*, shortly afterwards. At the same time, the growing shadows of international conflict brought the period of high Victorian optimism into which Trevelyan had been born to an end around the turn of the century. European troubles seemed to be threatening international peace and stability, indeed they seemed potentially to be threatening the global hegemony of Britain and the British Empire; and consciousness of this gave rise to an intensified concern with modern European history in Britain, a concern whose expression was to be very different from that of the long-lived Whig tradition represented by Trevelyan.

3

Open borders

If the French Revolution and its consequences dominated British historians' interest in Europe for most of the nineteenth century, then, as the century came to an end, their attention turned eastward towards Germany, the Habsburg Monarchy and the Balkans. This was not, initially at least, because of their past, but rather because of their present, and more threateningly still, perhaps, their future. The growing power and, for many thinking Britons, challenge of Germany, particularly with the construction of a high seas battle fleet, beginning in 1898, backed by a booming industrial economy and heralded by an ambitious and rhetorically aggressive monarch, Kaiser Wilhelm II, caused some historians to focus on the German past, as the unification of Germany at the beginning of the 1870s had already done in the case of Sir John Seeley. At the same time, however, British historians of Germany, as of France, were heavily dependent on the work of native scholars, whose view of the German past was almost uniformly positive and uncritical. Germany had devised the rules of modern historical scholarship, stressing objectivity of approach and neutrality of style and judgment, and British scholars were keen to demonstrate that they respected them. They undertook little original research themselves, but many knew German, and they were able to use published documentary collections and the works of leading German historians to familiarize an English-language readership with the past of the country that was now replacing France as the dominant and most ambitious power on the European Continent.

Not untypical, and among the most successful, was Sir John Marriott, whose textbook *The Remaking of Modern Europe, 1789–1878*, published in 1909, reached its 21st edition by 1933. Marriott also wrote *The Problem of German History*, published in 1911. He was essentially a disciple of the German nationalist or Borussian school of History, almost inevitably perhaps, since his account of German history rested largely on its work and embodied no original research. Thus Marriot declared that 'the long delayed but splendidly achieved consummation of German unity by the national uprising of 1871' was 'the crown and climax of German history ... At last, Germany has attained to nationhood; at last the German people have a common fatherland.' The son of a Manchester solicitor and, for much of his life, a History Tutor in Oxford, Marriott gained his views on Continental European history at second hand. 'Historians', he remarked disarmingly in his autobiography, 'may be divided into two classes: expositors and researchers, those who devote themselves to investigating the sources, and those who popularize the results thus obtained ... Circumstances have combined with my inclinations to make me an expositor rather than a research worker.' Marriott read and spoke French and German, and visited Germany and Austria a number of times from 1883 onwards; but he knew them only as a tourist. He went to the opera at Bayreuth on one occasion, but found Wagner tedious, and he disliked France because of the poor quality of its golf courses. 'It is not', he remarked in his autobiography, 'on my holidays abroad that my fondest memories dwell.'

Marriott did indeed spend much of his leisure time from 1899 onwards on the golf course. He was a Tory MP and a frequent contributor to the weeklies on questions of the day: those that interested him were, despite his authorship of what was for a long time regarded as the standard treatment of the diplomacy of the Eastern Question (1917), domestic, notably the financing of the railways. He also ran a successful summer school in Oxford, at which almost 200 Germans were present in July 1914, causing him considerable difficulties before he could get them safely away. But this, with his holiday encounters, was about the extent of his contact with Germans as people. As a practised public speaker he gained a reputation as an exciting and popular lecturer at Oxford, and, though not an immodest man, he claimed with some justification to possess the qualities of 'lucidity and accuracy' in his historical works. 'I should never', he wrote, 'have become an historian had I not been convinced that history is of high political utility, and that it cannot perform that service unless it be approached in a scientific spirit . . . If we can trace effects to their causes, we ought to get some guidance in the conduct of contemporary affairs.' Yet remarkably, his autobiography, published in 1946, shortly after his death at the age of eighty-five, and covering a period marked by, among other things, two World Wars and the rise and fall of Fascism and Nazism, makes no mention of foreign countries apart from holiday trips. Nor do his books attempt to draw any lessons from history. In 1915, in collaboration with Sir Charles Grant Robertson (1869–1948), he wrote *The Evolution of Prussia*, which bore few traces of the conflict during which it was written and remained unaltered through successive editions up to the aftermath of the Second World War.

Marriott was far more characteristic than Trevelyan of the historians of his time, with their general belief in objectivity, neutrality and scholarly rigour. Sir Adolphus Ward's three-volume *Germany 1815–1890*, for instance, breathed a tone, as one reviewer noted, of 'serene detachment' and 'absolute impartiality' despite being published at the height of the First World War. Unlike Marriott, Ward was steeped in German history and culture: he had been brought up in Germany as the son of the British Consul in Leipzig and Hamburg, was bilingual in English and German, and his works were sufficiently well known in Germany itself for him to be given an honorary degree from Leipzig University. He wrote virtually all the entries on Germany in the *Cambridge Modern History*, and was awarded a Prussian knighthood in 1911. Other historians who concerned themselves directly with German history and were therefore deeply upset by the outbreak of the war either kept silent or maintained, like Ward, a stance of studied neutrality in their books. Above all, British historians did not try to look back very far into German history for an explanation of the war and Germany's conduct of it. Sir Charles Grant Robertson's biography *Bismarck*, for instance, published in 1918, was completely neutral in tone and drew no lines of causation between the unification of Germany and the outbreak of the First World War.

II

It was not immediately in Germany, however, but in the Balkans that the First World War broke out. By the turn of the century it was becoming clear that the Habsburg Monarchy, along with the Ottoman Empire, was in a state of ferment, though not yet, perhaps, of terminal decay, with subject national minorities struggling for their rights and striving for national autonomy. English liberals were temperamentally inclined to look on such movements with sympathy. G. M. Trevelyan was one of many who took up the cause of the Balkan nationalities, notably the Serbs. Most notable of all, however, was Robert (R. W.) Seton-Watson (1879–1951). Originally, and already somewhat unconventionally, intending to study the German Reformation, Seton-Watson became seriously interested in nationality problems in the Habsburg Monarchy during a visit to Vienna. He championed the rights of subject groups like the Czechs and Romanians, and began to write polemical books and pamphlets denouncing attempts by the German and, especially, the Hungarian authorities, in their respective halves of the Dual Monarchy, to curtail their linguistic, cultural and political rights. During the First World War he played a pivotal part in bringing about the collapse of the Habsburg Monarchy and, especially, the independence of Czechoslovakia. This was politics rather than history, but in East-Central Europe and the Balkans, the two were inextricably bound up together. When Seton-Watson later founded the School of Slavonic and East European Studies at the University of London, he made sure that it included a Department of History. He brought up his sons in a cosmopolitan, multilingual home environment, and, not surprisingly, one of them, Hugh, became a distinguished historian of Russia and Eastern Europe, and another, Christopher, of modern Italy: a rare though, as we shall see later on, not unique example of family influence leading to a preoccupation with European history.

At the same time, interest in Russian history was also beginning to emerge, led in particular by Bernard (later Sir Bernard) Pares (1867–1949). Late in life, he claimed to have nurtured a passion for things Russian already as a child, but his son Richard, himself a distinguished historian, considered that this was a retrospective construction. A man of independent means, supported by the wealth of his provincial banking family, Bernard Pares read Classics at Cambridge, not very successfully, and on graduating went on a kind of one-man Grand Tour of the Continent. He travelled to Dieppe, and thence to Paris, where he attended lectures and seminars and taught himself French, mainly through reading with a dictionary. Moving eastwards, he studied at Heidelberg, Berlin and Dresden, visited Austria and Hungary, and spent six months in Italy, where he conceived an admiration for Garibaldi and indeed inspired G. M. Trevelyan, a family friend, with the same passion. By this stage in his travels, Pares had also acquired a good working knowledge of German and Italian. He initially went to Russia in 1898 in order to visit the Napoleonic battlefields. 'He had', wrote his son, 'a passion for battlefields, especially those of Napoleon, and would speak of them in the same tones in which other connoisseurs might have spoken of a vintage claret.' He had seen all the others, and none now remained to visit but the Russian. Once in Russia, however, he fell under the spell of the Russian peasantry, who seemed to him so much more honest and open than what his son called 'the depressed yokels of Surrey and Cambridgeshire'. He also arrived at a time when liberal politics were beginning to stir, leading to the establishment of parliamentary institutions and political parties a few years later during the 1905 Revolution. Pares duly learned Russian, struck up an acquaintance, which he deepened in the following years, with a variety of Russian liberals, then returned to Britain to teach adult education classes on Modern European History, including the French Revolution, Napoleon, the unification of Italy and Germany, and, only later on, Russia.

Pares was appointed Reader, then Professor of Russian History, at the University of Liverpool – the first in the United Kingdom. He visited Russia repeatedly, and wrote extensively about contemporary Russian politics, much as Seton-Watson wrote about contemporary politics in East-Central Europe. During the First World War, he spent three and a half years in Russia, in an entirely unofficial capacity; he supported the Provisional Government after the Revolution of 1917 and later the 'Whites' who were attempting to roll back the tide of Bolshevism after Lenin had come to power. Cut off from the country by the triumph of Communism, he moved to the School of Slavonic Studies in London and in 1926 published *A History of Russia*, which for a long time remained the standard work in English. Only in the mid-1930s did he return to the country, and during the Second World War, following Hitler's invasion of Russia in 1941, he became a popular and widely read advocate of the Anglo-Soviet alliance. Like Seton-Watson, indeed like a whole generation of British scholars who focused on Europe in the early to mid twentieth century, Pares was as much a man of action as a scholar – no researcher, but a great synthesizer, someone whose interest in the European past was directly inspired by, and inextricably linked with, the increasingly violent and chaotic European present.

III

These linkages between European – and especially Central and East European – politics and European history were particularly strong during and after the First World War. To begin with, the First World War did not shatter historians' belief in the accuracy and objectivity of their profession. Ramsay Muir (1872–1941), Professor of Modern History at Manchester, in his book *Britain's Case Against Germany*, published in 1914, was simply stating the creed of the historians of his day when he wrote: 'I have honestly tried . . . to see the facts plainly, and never to tamper with them.' *Why We are at War*, published by a group of Oxford History Tutors in September 1914, consisted largely of documentary extracts translated from German and French, rather as if it was intended to provide the basis for a university Special Subject. However, both these books were of course designed to serve a propaganda purpose, selecting and interpreting the documents so as to pin the blame for the war on the Germans and convince readers that the Germans had committed terrible atrocities. The fact that German historians were producing precisely the same kind of documentary editions, books and pamphlets designed to justify the German entry into the war, defend the German conduct of the war, and convict the

British of atrocities of their own, notably overseas, in their running of the British Empire, did not wholly undermine this belief in the ultimate arbitrating power of documents. After the war was over, historians in both countries redoubled their efforts to unearth, publish and analyse as many documents as possible relating to the origins of the war. Vast, multi-volume histories of the war and editions of foreign policy papers poured off the presses. If only everything could be discovered and published, the truth might finally be known.

Such was the urgency and importance of this subject that diplomatic history, the history of international relations, quickly became the most prestigious and best-funded branch of modern history in the interwar period. British historians became interested in Continental countries not because they set a good, or a bad, example for the British, or because they demonstrated the universality of British liberal principles, or because they taught lessons that British history did not, but because their history had suddenly impacted on that of the United Kingdom in the most brutal and dramatic way possible, in a World War, and therefore badly needed to be understood. This was not new, of course: in the mid to late-Victorian era, historians who realized that almost all British Foreign Office mandarins had been educated in Oxford or Cambridge drew the conclusion that they ought to know something about the 'Great Powers' of the European Continent before they graduated. What was new in the interwar period was a focus not on the internal history of these countries, but instead on their external relations, which in some respects, it was argued, lived a life of their own, determined by the European 'system' of international relations.

New courses were duly established in British universities, along with new Chairs; the Chair of Modern History at Cambridge, founded in 1930, was a typical example of this trend. Its first incumbent was Harold Temperley (1879–1939), a somewhat austere figure of whom his biographer remarks that 'from the beginning Harold seemed far more capable of romantic attachment to artifacts, literature, and ideas than to women'. Temperley studied with Acton in Cambridge, and clearly fell under his influence. Starting out as a specialist in early nineteenth-century English history, Temperley was awakened to the importance of Central Europe and the Balkans by the nationality conflicts in the Habsburg Empire, which he toured in 1907 and again in 1909, and returning to the Balkans in 1910. Typical of English liberals in their various hues, he conceived a passion for upholding the rights of oppressed ethnic minorities in the region. Invalided out of the army during the war, he wrote a positive history of Serbia (he did not, his biographer remarks, dwell on the 'unsavoury' aspects of the Serbian past), as a result of which he was drafted into the British delegation to the Paris Peace Conference. This made him a diplomatic historian: he wrote a multi-volume history of the Conference, and then began work on an extensive collection of documents on the origins of the war. In his Inaugural Lecture as Professor of Modern History at Cambridge, he declared that progress in historical research was made only 'by limiting aims, by increasing objectivity, and by abandoning vain speculation'. The editing of diplomatic documents seemed to be the best way of achieving these aims in the history of international relations.

In this enterprise, Temperley found a ready collaborator in George Peabody Gooch (1873–1968), whose books, too numerous to mention, dealt with a wide variety of topics in British and European history, from lives of Louis XV and Catherine the Great to studies of international relations in the prewar and interwar years – many of them, particularly those dealing with the eighteenth century, works of popular history written in his old age. In his youth and prime, however, Gooch's approach to history was closely interlinked with his political activities and his relations with the British Foreign Office. Gooch was born in London, into an upper middle-class, Anglican family whose considerable wealth had been earned in the City. He went to Eton, but disliked its lack of intellectual and religious seriousness, and went after only three years to King's College, London, at the age of fifteen, for pre-university studies.

This strengthened his Anglicanism, and when he matriculated at Trinity College, Cambridge, he quickly made an impression as 'a prodigy of learning', to quote his contemporary the later novelist John Cowper Powys, who went on to remark: 'the man's learning was something monstrous . . . There was indeed something about it that was morbid and unnatural.' Gooch was influenced by Seeley's insistence that the study of history was linked to the pursuit of politics in the present, and by Acton, whose moral seriousness did a good deal to deepen Gooch's own. Both steered his interests towards the history of the European Continent. In 1895 he went to Berlin, where he heard Treitschke lecture but was unimpressed when he listened in to a debate in the Reichstag: the liberal opposition, he thought, was feeble and old-fashioned; he read all the major German historians and from this point onwards regarded Germany as his 'second country'. Indeed, it was on this visit that he met his future wife, a young German art student, whom he married in 1903.

On his return to Cambridge, Gooch formed a close friendship with Acton in the Regius Professor's last years but took his lack of productivity as a warning and reacted strongly against it; some might say, indeed, he reacted against it to excess. Acton taught him to insist on historical objectivity unaffected by the passing political concerns of the day, but he also reinforced his belief in the study of history as an essentially moral, and moralizing, pursuit. Despite Acton's backing, however, Gooch was turned down for a fellowship at Trinity College. For the rest of his life he lived off his family income, his father having died when Gooch was fifteen, leaving him more than enough means to support himself independently and employ a small army of domestic servants to look after him. In any case, many of his publications proved so successful that there was never the remotest threat of his having to get a university job. Instead, his conscience drove him into adult education for working men, into work for the London City Mission, and into campaigns for the temperance movement (he was a lifelong teetotaller). In 1906 he became MP for Bath in the Liberal Party landslide of that year but lost his seat in 1910.

Gooch made his reputation as a historian with a large book on *History and Historians in the 19th Century*, published in 1913. A learned and comprehensive survey covering several countries and many topics, it put forward the view that the Germans, Ranke in the lead, were the real creators of modern historical scholarship. He was more critical of the French, whose accounts of the Revolution he regarded as partisan (on one side or the other), and the British – he particularly disliked Carlyle, though he admitted the stimulus he had given to historical study. Reviewers were quick to notice his application of Actonian principles. 'Acton himself', one of them said, 'had he written the book, would no doubt have been more profound, but his profundity would have prevented him from ever writing it.' Gooch argued that historians had to have integrity, balance of judgment, expertise and the command of the correct methods of source-criticism, and they had to avoid determinism at all costs, recognizing that human beings possessed free will.

Both during and after the First World War, Gooch urged resistance to the propaganda of hate against Germany. As Editor of the *Contemporary Review* from 1911, he opened its columns to pacifists, though his disapproval of the German violation of Belgian neutrality prevented him from joining them. In 1919 he wrote:

> In the hurricane of rage which had swept over us owing to Germany's methods of waging war we have been tempted to extend our condemnation from William II to Bismarck and Frederick the Great, and to credit them with a double dose of original sin. Our reputation for sanity and scholarship depends on resisting the distorting passions of war.

As this suggests, he disapproved of the illiberalism and militarism of the Kaiser's Germany. And he also opposed nationalism, which he thought had 'fostered savage racial passions and repulsive national arrogance'. So he thought the punitive nature of the Versailles Treaty outrageous, and backed the League of Nations. He edited, with the ubiquitous Sir Adolphus Ward, the three-volume *Cambridge History of British Foreign Policy* and wrote the sections on 1902–19, when he criticized the Triple Entente as restricting Britain's freedom of action, while at the same time condemning the 'criminal levity' of Wilhelm II in the crisis of 1914 and pinning a good deal of the blame on the Austrian ultimatum to Serbia. Nevertheless, he argued, it was the Russian mobilization that precipitated the World War, while the British government did its best to stop the catastrophe, unsuccessfully because of the treaty obligations by which it was bound. Gooch deepened this analysis in his books *Recent Revelations of European Diplomacy* (1927) and *History of Modern Europe 1878–1919* (1923).

All this implied support for the Weimar Republic, which Gooch articulated in his volume on Germany in a general history of the modern world, published in 1925. The Republic, he warned, would need understanding and consideration from its neighbours if it were to survive; events such as the French occupation of the Ruhr in 1923 were profoundly dangerous. Not surprisingly, the book was translated into German the same year. All these works, coupled with Gooch's reputation as an even-handed historian of international relations, led to his appointment by his admirer, the first Labour Prime Minister, Ramsay MacDonald, as Editor-in-Chief, with Temperley, of a multi-volume work, *British Documents on the Origins of the War, 1898–1914*, for the Foreign Office. This fifteen-year project set the pattern of publication for the successful diplomatic historian of the 1930s and the postwar years, when other, similar series of documents were published under official auspices: books about British foreign policy linked to current concerns about international relations; histories of one or more of the countries with which Britain had dealings, particularly Germany; and the editorship of official documentary publications in the same field. Gooch supported appeasement, supposing like many that it would undermine Hitler's position in Germany, but from the outset he detested Nazi antisemitism and indeed, in 1934, he and his German wife severed all contacts with the German Embassy in London. He abandoned appeasement in the spring of 1939 after the final German invasion of rump Czecho-Slovakia, and supported the war from his retirement. At the same time, he refused to blame the German people as a whole for the crimes of Nazism, and indeed stuck to this line all the way up to his death at the age of ninety-five.

IV

Gooch and Temperley were perhaps the two most prominent of the diplomatic historians of the interwar years, but there were many others who built successful careers for themselves too, notably Sir Charles Webster (1886–1961), the first Stevenson Professor of International History at the London School of Economics, who wrote mainly on British foreign policy, took part in the Paris Peace Conference, and divided his time between the Foreign Office and academia. The combination of man of action and historian could be found in a younger generation, too: a particularly striking example was J. W. (Sir John) Wheeler-Bennett (1902–75), whose career owed much to the patronage of General Neill

Malcolm, sometime head of the British military mission in Berlin. Shell-shocked in an air-raid on his school in 1916, Wheeler-Bennett spoke with a stammer for much of his life, and was not considered fit for active service. Instead, he was found a position as Malcolm's unpaid Personal Assistant, then worked for the League of Nations Union and the international relations think-tank, Chatham House (Chairman: Neill Malcolm). In 1929 Malcolm persuaded him to go to Germany as an observer. Wheeler-Bennett had enough money to buy a small horse-breeding establishment, and the stud allowed him to mix freely and intimately with the German aristocracy and political elite, whose acquaintance he extended by running a kind of salon at his rooms in the Hotel Kaiserhof in Berlin. *Persona non grata* with the Nazis, he escaped death during the 'Night of the Long Knives' only through the chance that he was in Switzerland at the time; his rooms were raided by stormtroopers and he did not return. Instead, he began to write works of contemporary history in which he used his extensive personal knowledge of the participants to vivid effect, including a highly critical account of the German army (*The Nemesis of Power*), a biography of Hindenburg (*The Wooden Titan*) and a history of the making of the Treaty of Brest-Litovsk that had sealed Russia's withdrawal from the war early in 1918 (*The Forgotten Peace*). During the Second World War he worked for the Foreign Office; afterwards, he took up a research position in Oxford, where he acted as a mentor to a new generation of historians, more than one of whom began his career as his research assistant.

A similar historical, though rather different political, trajectory can be found in the career of Edward Hallett

(E. H.) Carr (1890–1982), who came into contact with Russia while working in the Foreign Office on liaison between the two countries during the First World War. He too played a role, albeit a junior one, in the 1919 Peace Settlement, and afterwards was posted to Riga, a backwater where life was so uneventful that he passed much of the time by learning Russian. During the 1920s and early 1930s Carr read his way through the great works of Russian literature, and began writing books on it in his spare time, notably *The Romantic Exiles*, published in 1933. Like many other British Russianists, as we shall see, he therefore in a sense came to Russian history through Russian literature. But he had of course experienced the 1917 Revolutions himself, even if only from the vantage-point of the British Foreign Office, and they proved a source of lasting fascination that eventually became an obsession. After leaving the Foreign Office, Carr taught at the world's first Department of International Relations, at the University of Wales, Aberystwyth.

Here he published a theoretical work on *The Twenty Years' Crisis*, designed to provide a 'realist' underpinning for the policy of appeasement, published, somewhat inopportunely, in 1939. His involvement in public life, typical of the diplomatic historians, continued through his employment during the war as a leader-writer for *The Times*, in which capacity he not only repeatedly advocated close collaboration with the Soviet Union but also argued that its institutions, or something very like them, offered the best prospect for the future of mankind. As a historian, his major work was a fourteen-volume *History of Soviet Russia*, which in fact only went up to the beginnings of Stalin's rule in the early 1930s.

It was remarkable for editing out almost all the uncertainties and conflicts that had accompanied the 1917 Revolution and its aftermath. Carr's interest was in history's winners, among whom he included the Soviets, not in its losers. On the other hand, his account of Soviet history was completely unacceptable to the Soviets themselves, since it could not really be called Marxist, let alone Leninist or Stalinist, in any meaningful sense. Based in Cambridge until his death, Carr exercised an influence on more than one generation of British historians of Soviet Russia.

In the same generation as Carr, another Russianist, Benedict (B. H.) Sumner (1893–1951) also came to History through his participation in the 1919 Peace Conference. Unlike Carr, Sumner had already learned Russian at school. After serving on the Western Front in Military Intelligence, he took up Diplomatic History and was closely involved with the Royal Institute of International Affairs, at Chatham House. Sumner's first major book, *Russia and the Balkans 1870–80* (1937), reflected exactly the wider interest among British historians in this part of Europe; drawing on printed, and a few manuscript, sources in many languages, it was a *tour de force* of detailed scholarship. In 1944, Sumner published a reflective *Survey of Russian History*, and in 1949 his study *Peter the Great and the Ottoman Empire* appeared. By this time, he was spending much of his time on carrying out the duties of Warden of All Souls College, Oxford. Like Carr, he had little close personal knowledge of Russia; indeed, he only paid one visit to the country, in 1930.

Not all the diplomatic historians entangled themselves in policymaking as Carr and his predecessors and contemporaries did. Perhaps the most famous of them all was too left-wing, too hostile to the 'Establishment' (a term he claimed the credit for inventing) and in general too contrary to find favour in government circles. Alan – universally known as A. J. P. – Taylor (1906–90) also belonged to the world of diplomatic history as it emerged to become the queen of historical disciplines between the wars. He grew up in a well-to-do but determinedly left-wing family in the North, and travelled several times with one or both of his parents to Italy, France and Germany as a child. After reading Modern History at Oxford, he was articled to a solicitor, but was so bored that he went back to Oxford to take up History again, although without enrolling for any courses. His old tutor, G. N. (later Sir George) Clark (1890–1979), told him: 'If you are going to be an historian, you must know German.' Weimar Germany seemed to Taylor, who had visited Soviet Russia and come back with largely positive impressions, an enticingly progressive place, but his attempts to make contacts with scholars there came to nothing and he was soon back where he had begun, still looking for a topic of research.

It is hard not to feel at this point that the senior historians at Oxford were doing everything they could to send the irritating and troublesome Taylor as far away from the university as possible. When he consulted the Regius Professor, H. W. C. Davis (1874–1928), Taylor received the advice to go to Vienna, which at the time, in the late 1920s, with the radical social policies pursued by the municipality that gave it the sobriquet 'Red Vienna', Taylor thought was an even more left-wing place than Berlin. Davis himself had a strong interest in European history, and had written a study of the political thought of Heinrich von Treitschke; he had also served on the British delegation to the Paris Peace Conference at the end of the First World War and knew many European historians and diplomats. He suggested that 'my old friend' A. F. Pribram would be able to supervise Taylor's doctorate. Pribram had made something of a name for himself in England as an expert on Oliver Cromwell, and Taylor thought vaguely of doing a project on the history of English radicalism. He duly wrote to the great man, got a welcoming response, and went straight to Austria, travelling and staying in some luxury thanks to the generosity of his wealthy parents.

But Pribram by this time had deserted English history for international relations and was working on the origins of the First World War, converted to this topic, like so many other historians, by the cataclysmic experience of the war itself. He thought Taylor would do better to work on the history of international relations – in particular between the early Victorian English Radicals, on whom Taylor had written an unsuccessful prize essay at Oxford, and their Viennese counterparts. Pribram gave him a list of books on Austrian history and told him to come back when he had read them; Taylor duly learned German by reading doggedly through them and looking up every word in the dictionary, then receiving some private tuition, and finally, and probably most usefully, acquiring an Austrian girlfriend. He saw Pribram again, and on his advice began working on mid-nineteenth-century diplomatic history; the relations between English and Austrian radicals had been minimal and hardly generated any source material. Instead, Pribram pushed him into working on broader aspects of Anglo-Austrian diplomatic relations in the period, and after trawling through innumerable documents in French and German, Taylor came up with a topic, and duly completed a book, *The Italian Problem in European Diplomacy, 1847–1849*, published in 1934. Finding the formalities too daunting, he never did register for a doctorate, and by the time the book was published, in any case, he had become a Lecturer at Manchester University, responsible for teaching the whole of modern European history, largely on the recommendation of Pribram, who had visited England shortly before to deliver the Ford Lectures at Oxford.

Taylor continued his career as a diplomatic historian after the war, culminating in his brilliant synoptic survey of nineteenth-century European diplomacy, *The Struggle for Mastery in Europe* (1954), but he also wrote a short history of the Habsburg Monarchy and, more controversially, a brief general history of Germany since the Middle Ages. First published in 1945, this book had its origins in an essay on the Weimar Republic written at the behest of the Political Warfare Executive, as part of a compilation 'being put together', as Taylor later remarked, 'in order to explain to the conquerors what sort of country they were conquering'. The piece was rejected (because it was, Taylor thought, 'too depressing') and so he expanded it into a short book, *The Course of German History* (1946). It was indeed rabidly anti-German, but, more interestingly perhaps, it reflected the fact that Taylor was above all a diplomatic historian by arguing that German history was determined not by internal social, cultural or political factors, but by Germany's inability to find a settled place in Europe. Taylor built up a wholly deterministic geopolitical argument that purported to demonstrate how Germany was inevitably driven by a permanent lust for conquest and domination: 'Every German frontier is artificial, therefore impermanent; that is the permanence of German geography.' All the platitudes and clichés of British wartime propaganda about the German national character were wheeled out in the book, but they were subordinated time and again to an essentially geopolitical mode of explanation: 'If a natural cataclysm had placed a broad sea between the Germans and the French, the German character would not have been dominated by militarism . . . The German character was determined by their geographical position.' So wedded was Taylor to this kind of argument that, even in 1961, in the Preface to the second edition of the book, he still saw Germany – defeated, divided and, in the western part at least, democratic though it was – as a threat: 'I have almost reached the point of believing that I shall not live to see a third German war; but events have an awkward trick of running in the wrong direction, just when you least expect it.'

V

The Course of German History, which Taylor later admitted was his weakest book, demonstrated in the end the inability of the diplomatic historians, in the last analysis even including Carr, to come up with a balanced, informed and convincing account of the history of individual modern European states (Taylor's last major work, his classic *English History 1914–45*, published in 1965, was the exception, born of decades of personal experience and participant observation). Yet this did not mean that British historians, whether they were interested in international relations or not, were unfamiliar either with the Continent or with the nature of historical studies there. It is clear, for instance, that his youthful experience in Austria was central to Taylor's formation as a historian; it was Pribram, for example, who taught him to lecture without notes, and Pribram's former colleague Heinrich Friedjung whose books provided the model for Taylor's own. Travels in East-Central Europe aroused in Taylor a lasting interest in the region and its history. When he spoke German, it was with a strong Viennese accent. Taylor liked to portray his own personal history as a chapter of accidents, but in all that he did he was to a degree following, or participating in, a broader trend. Just as they had done before the First World War, so too in the 1920s, many British historians made their way to Germany and Austria to receive the professional historical training they found it so difficult to obtain at home. The PhD indeed was only generally introduced in Britain after the First World War, partly in an attempt to reduce the German influence on British historical scholarship. It was not until the advent of the Nazis in Germany and the creation of the Dollfuss dictatorship in Austria that the flow of British historians to Germany more or less came to an end.

The principles of *Quellenkritik* (source-criticism), the institution of the research seminar, the very idea of History as a scientific discipline, all of this was to be found above all in Germany, and, for medievalists, to a lesser extent at the École des Chartes in Paris. Taylor himself was friendly with the medievalist Geoffrey Barraclough (1908–84), who studied with Karl Alexander von Müller in Berlin, and knew others who were studying in Germany or Austria too; Barraclough's books in the 1930s focused on the medieval Papacy and did not concern themselves directly with Germany, but he clearly felt Germany was the place to get a training in the subject. Among British historians who studied in Germany, usefully listed in an Appendix to Stuart Wallace's book *War and the Image of Germany: British Academics 1914–1918* (1988), were the economic historian W. J. Ashley, who was at Göttingen in 1880; J. B. Bury, who was there in the same year; J. H. Clapham, who studied at Paris as well as at Göttingen; the medievalist G. G. Coulton, an alumnus of Heidelberg; H. W. C. Davis, who went to Dresden; H. A. L. Fisher, who moved from Paris in 1889 to Berlin the following year; A. G. Little, who was at Dresden and Göttingen in the mid-1880s; Ramsay Muir, who left it rather late (1914) to go to Marburg; R. W. Seton-Watson, who was at Berlin, Vienna and Paris in 1903–6; the economic historian George Unwin, at Berlin in 1898; and the diplomatic historian E. L. (later, Sir Llewellyn) Woodward, who was at Darmstadt in 1912. Mostly they enrolled for just one or two semesters, but a few, like Taylor, went for longer: the medievalist R. L. Poole, for example, stayed long enough to receive a PhD from Leipzig in 1882. In the late nineteenth and early twentieth centuries, German historical scholarship exercised a huge influence on how British historians approached British as well as European history, and undergraduates in an increasing number of universities, led above all by Manchester, were trained in German historical methods.

This was part of a trend that affected many different topics, including, in particular, Chemistry and Medicine. As the Oxford historian A. J. Carlyle had remarked in 1911, the 'position of the great German nation in philosophy, science

and literature was so powerful that students were bound
to study German and go to Germany if they were of any
promise'. A training in Economic History hardly seemed to
be complete before 1914 without a stint in a German seminar.
More generally, although the First World War created something of a rupture in this exchange, German ways of doing
history remained dominant in a large part of the British historical profession for some years after the war, their influence
diminished but not entirely destroyed by the obvious parti-
sanship of German historians themselves in the propaganda
war that accompanied the real fighting in 1914–18 and indeed
lasted well beyond it. To be taught by men who had studied in
Germany, spoke and wrote German as well as French, knew
Central Europe well, and maintained a wide network of contacts amongst their fellow-historians in the region meant for
some historians, like Taylor, inevitably to be influenced in the
direction of European History.

In an era of dictatorship, conflict and war, research
in Europe was well-nigh impossible, and contacts, especially
with Central European historians, difficult to maintain. In
the 1930s, however, traffic began in the other direction. A
number of historians, particularly Jewish historians, were
forced to flee the growing antisemitism of Central European
states, above all Nazi Germany. Concerned groups of British
university teachers successfully found them jobs or provided financial support. The refugees included the Ancient
History specialist Viktor Ehrenburg; the medievalist Hans
Liebeschütz; the nineteenth-century specialist Erich Eyck;
the biographer of Engels, Gustav Mayer; and the early medievalist Wilhelm Levison. Their financial circumstances were

often shaky: Erich Eyck, for example, was only able to survive because his wife ran a boarding-house in London, though he was invited to give the occasional lecture in Oxford. Others – a considerably larger number – were unable to get support in Britain and emigrated more or less rapidly to the USA, including Fritz Epstein, Hajo Holborn, Ernst Kantorowicz, George Mosse, Hans Rosenberg and Hans Rothfels. A few of those who stayed in Britain did so because they had themselves researched and published on British history, like Levison, Mayer or Eyck. All of them, however, had already reached their maturity as historians before they arrived, and essentially carried on what they had been doing before in a new academic setting. Levison's Ford Lectures were delivered in English and published in 1946 as *England and the Continent in the Eighth Century*, and Eyck's books on Pitt and Fox, and on Gladstone, did find an English publisher, but Mayer's two-volume – and for many decades standard – biography of Frederick Engels, who after all was a figure of English as much as of German history, remained untranslated and so found very few readers in the UK.

Not all those who came to Britain from Central Europe came as refugees. Eric Hobsbawm, for example, who was born in Alexandria in 1917 and grew up in Vienna and Berlin, was a British citizen, and his uncle – with whom he had been living after the death of his father and mother in, respectively, 1929 and 1931 – took the family to England, by a fortunate chance, mainly for business reasons, just as Hitler was coming to power. Aleady by the time he became an undergraduate at Cambridge, Hobsbawm spoke several European languages, including French, Spanish and Italian.

His refusal to resign from the Communist Party despite his growing estrangement from it after 1956 reflected not least his feeling that to do so would betray the school friends in Berlin who had stayed in Germany and been imprisoned, tortured and killed by the Nazis. Like most of his generation, he did not begin to write on history until after the Second World War, and when he did, his work focused on agrarian movements, labour and trade unions, and what he called 'primitive rebels', from Italy to East Anglia, Spain and Latin America. As a Marxist, albeit of an independent stamp that never toed the Communist Party's intellectual line, Hobsbawm addressed the big questions and had a gift for marshalling disparate material in the service of large and challenging generalizations, from the 'general crisis of the seventeenth century' to the periodization of the twentieth; his most widely read works were thematic and analytical surveys of *The Age of Revolution*, *The Age of Capital*, *The Age of Empire* and *Age of Extremes*, covering European (and to a far lesser extent, world) history from 1789 to the present.

British historians born and brought up abroad, like Hobsbawm, or for that matter Lord Acton and Sir Lewis Namier (1888–1960) who had come to England before the First World War to escape antisemitism in his native Poland, had always been amongst those who had concerned themselves with the European Continent. They were relatively few in number. But in the postwar years a whole group of foreign-born historians began to emerge on the scene. Born in German-speaking parts of Europe in the years preceding the Nazi seizure of power, and mostly Jewish by origin, they had been forced to flee the Third Reich, or to leave parts of Europe conquered by the Nazis. Some came over with their parents or were sent over from Europe as part of a scheme to take Jewish children out of danger – the so-called *Kindertransporte*. They received their university training and in some cases also their schooling in the UK, so that many of them became historians, in other words, as a result of their education in this country. They included the medievalists Walter Ullmann and Karl Leyser, the cultural historian Nicolai Rubinstein, the early modernist Helli (H. G.) Koenigsberger, the diplomatic historian and later chronicler of the German-Jewish economic elite Werner Mosse, the historian of Victorian politics Edgar Feuchtwanger, and the analyst of early German and Austrian antisemitism Peter Pulzer. Many of them, particularly if they entered the British army, or if they found their German name made getting a job too difficult, took British names: Siegfried Pollak became Sidney Pollard, Ernst Peter Henoch became Peter Hennock, Gottfried Ehrenburg became Geoffrey Elton, Hans Gubrauer became John Grenville.

Often they had to find their way into academic life through considerable difficulties. John Grenville, middle-class son of a lawyer whose fortune had been destroyed in the prewar inflation, left Germany in 1939 on a *Kindertransport* at the age of ten. After just over two years at a boarding school, where he learned English and became, by his own account, a passable slow left-arm bowler, Grenville, at the age of thirteen, was taken out of school by the children's refugee committee, who would not allow him to get an academic education despite his father's support for it, but expected him to enter a trade. His scientific training at the Cambridgeshire Technical School, another boarding institution, was not successful: he got chemical poisoning and was told to get an outdoor job to recover. So he became under-gardener at Peterhouse, where he read voraciously in History in his spare time. 'My request for permission to use the Peterhouse library', he wrote later, 'caused consternation. I was finally given permission, but only on condition that I would not attempt to enter Cambridge University as a student.' The Master was sufficiently amazed by a College gardener reading books to arrange a weekly session over cocoa and biscuits at which they discussed what Grenville had been reading. At eighteen, Grenville was accepted to read History in evening classes at Birkbeck College, London: on hearing the news that he was leaving, the Bursar of Peterhouse told him that the Fellows would have liked him to stay because, as he said, 'you have the makings of a Head Porter' (Grenville subsequently became Professor of Modern History at Birmingham University).

Others went through similar experiences, if not such quintessentially Cambridge ones: Willi Guttsmann (1920–98) also worked as a gardener before going to Birkbeck and then, like Grenville, on to the LSE; dropping the second 'n' from his German name to signify his new British identity, Guttsman became Librarian of the new University of East Anglia, where he published a series of important books on the history of German Social Democracy and particularly its cultural activities. Grenville's first book was on British foreign policy in the nineteenth century, and many others amongst this younger generation of émigré historians also worked on British history, including, for example, Pollard, Elton and Hennock: in the British historical profession of the time, it was still not easy to find a PhD supervisor on anything other than a topic in British domestic or diplomatic history. But sooner or later they gravitated naturally enough towards the history of the Continent they had been forced to leave: Elton wrote *Reformation Europe*, Hennock on the comparative study of health and disease in nineteenth-century Britain and Germany, Grenville on the history of Hamburg under the Nazis, Pollard on the industrialization of Europe, Feuchtwanger on Bismarckian Germany, and so on. This was important, because by the time they had secured academic posts for themselves, in the 1950s, they were in a position not only to teach Continental history but also to attract postgraduate students to research it.

Perhaps the best example of their impact can be found in the career of Francis (originally Franz Ludwig) Carsten (1911–98), whose surname at least was perhaps sufficiently easy for the English to pronounce for him to feel he had no need to change it. Carsten had become a Communist in Berlin in the early 1930s and been a member of a left-wing resistance group, the 'New Beginning', which sought to bridge the gap between Social Democrats and Communists under the Third Reich. The group was broken up by the Gestapo in 1935, and Carsten, who had a valid foreign passport, had to flee the country. Although he had a law degree, his career in the law had been stopped because he was Jewish; and in Dutch exile he also became disillusioned with the endless and futile squabbling of the émigré left-wing political milieu. He determined instead to research the origins of Prussia, to get at, as it were, the beginning of the story of Germany's descent into Nazism. He worked, unsupervised, on the Junker manorial economy in the early modern period, and published a couple of articles in academic journals in Holland in 1938–9.

This got him the backing of Sir George Clark, then Professor of Economic History in Oxford, who took on Carsten as a doctoral student. After working in the government's propaganda department during the war, Carsten got a lectureship at London University. When he got the post, he later wrote, 'there was no one in London who taught any German history, and very few university teachers outside London did so'.

Over the following forty years Carsten supervised a long series of research students of medieval, early modern and modern German history; for the first fifteen years or so after the war, he was virtually the only historian who did this; and, which was just as important, since he himself was an archival scholar, he ensured that his many doctoral students were too. This had an enormous impact in raising the standards of research in German History in this country, at a time when most historians who wrote about Germany had never even set foot in a German archive. At the same time, however, the roots of Carsten's work in a Social Democratic or Marxist interpretation of German history ensured that his books were not translated into German and, if they were reviewed at all, got highly critical notices from established historians in West Germany. By the 1960s his work had moved on to the Weimar Republic, and in 1964 he published, in German, an archivally based study of the army during the Weimar years, containing devastating revelations about the extent to which it had undermined the Republic. The book caused an enormous storm in West Germany, and was vehemently rejected by professional military historians; but it has stood the test of time and is still the standard work on the subject. Later, he wrote a comparative history of the 1918 Revolution in Germany and Austria and a study of Austrian Fascism, both also based on extensive archival research, before concluding his career by returning to his roots with biographies of leading German socialists and an account of the workers' resistance to Nazism.

VI

Both exiled Central European historians and British diplomatic history specialists were brought into the war effort in various ways. Francis Carsten, for example, was recruited to the Political Warfare Executive (where he was responsible for rejecting Alan Taylor's essay on the Weimar Republic not, he said, because it was too depressing, but simply because it was 'too full of mistakes'). Taylor himself gave propaganda broadcasts. Other British historians entered the intelligence service, a number of them, for example, being engaged in the analysis of decrypts at Bletchley Park. Such activities in some cases stimulated an interest in recent European and, especially, German history that otherwise would not have existed. The war ripped a number of dons away from their normal academic pursuits and plunged them into an unfamiliar, exciting and in many ways extraordinary world that they naturally wanted to write about after the war was over. Without his war work in the European Service of the BBC, for example, it is difficult to imagine how the Oxford historian Alan Bullock would have been inspired to write the first major biography of Hitler by either a British or a German historian. Similarly, F. W. D. (Bill) Deakin devoted himself to researching the Hitler–Mussolini relationship for his two volumes on *The Brutal Friendship* (1963), and his classic *The Embattled*

Mountain (1971), a book about the British expedition to Yugoslavia, in which he himself had played a leading role; the same sort of thing may be said of a whole range of other works by British historians in the 1950s and 1960s, for example C. M. (Monty) Woodhouse, whose involvement in the Greek resistance to Hitler turned him from a Classical scholar into a historian of modern Greece. Michael Balfour's books on German history, including *The Kaiser and his Times* (1964), emerged from his own experience as a senior civil servant in the postwar administration of the British zone of occupation; he began by writing a book about his experiences, then left the civil service to become an academic.

In parallel to the emergence of a whole generation of exiled European historians, therefore, there also emerged a whole generation of British historians of Europe who had been inspired to turn to the Continent as a result of their own experiences during the war. Some indeed were inspired by the war to change field entirely, most famously perhaps the Oxford Professor of Medieval History, Geoffrey Barraclough, who abandoned his work on the medieval Papacy because he no longer thought it relevant, and turned to studies of *Factors in German History* (1946) and *The Origins of Modern Germany* (1947), and in 1964 published *An Introduction to Contemporary History*; he did revisit the medieval Papacy in his sixties, but until the end of his career devoted much of his time to publishing on the recent past.

A good example of the impact of the Second World War on British historians is the career of Hugh Trevor-Roper, who trained in the 1930s as a historian of seventeenth-century England and published a highly critical biography of

Archbishop Laud in 1940, at the precocious age of twenty-six. A Student, or in other words, Fellow, of Christ Church, Oxford, he was recruited in 1940 to the intelligence service. A gifted linguist, he could read German, and so he was given the task of analysing intercepted German radio traffic. He impressed his superiors with his penetrating intellect, and in September 1945, when the secret service was asked to prepare a report on what had happened to Hitler, Trevor-Roper was commissioned to write it. The Russians had in fact discovered the charred remains of the Nazi leader outside the bunker in Berlin, but they kept this quiet so as to be able to embarrass the Western Allies: Stalin, indeed, even told them on one occasion that Hitler had escaped and was being sheltered by General Franco in Spain. Trevor-Roper took a small team to Germany, tracked down seven witnesses to the last week of Hitler's life in the bunker, located and read the diaries and letters of the participants, and established the basic outlines of what has since become the familiar story of the German leader's last days. The report was a triumph, and with the secret service's permission, Trevor-Roper turned it into a book, *The Last Days of Hitler*, which had sold half a million copies worldwide by 1983 and has remained continuously in print since its first publication in 1947.

Trevor-Roper's account of Nazi Germany was pioneering in many respects apart from its detailed revelations of life in the bunker. 'The structure of German politics and administration', wrote Trevor-Roper, 'instead of being, as the Nazis claimed, "pyramidal" and "monolithic", was in fact a confusion of private empires, private armies, and private intelligence services.' Nothing was 'rationally centralized'.

Hitler, far from being the tool of particular interests, was a charismatic dictator who held the entire leadership of Nazi Germany in thrall to his personality. Nazism was a genuine, if repulsive and intellectually vapid, ideology; from the beginning, Hitler was hell-bent on the conquest of Russia, the extermination of the Slavs, and the colonization of the East. He aimed ultimately at 'world-power or ruin'; he was a revolutionary, though his revolution was one of destruction rather than construction; he was not a conservative in any sense of the word. All these arguments have stood the test of time, despite periodic attempts in the intervening decades to upset them. The book established Trevor-Roper overnight as a leading historian of Nazi Germany.

In this capacity, Trevor-Roper used his contacts to obtain and publish in 1953 an English translation – not by himself – of *Hitler's Table Talk*, the Nazi Leader's lunch- and dinnertime monologues, and subsequently he was asked on many occasions by publishers to write introductions to other newly discovered documents such as a portion of the diaries of Joseph Goebbels acquired on the so-called 'grey market' from an East German source. In 1956 this work, together with his publications on seventeenth-century England and his undoubted Conservative Party sympathies, landed him the post of Regius Professor of Modern History at Oxford. During the 1950s and 1960s, he wrote widely on the history of the Continent, including studies of the rise of Christianity, very much in the sceptical spirit of Edward Gibbon, and, in particular, of the phenomenon of witchcraft in the early modern era. Trevor-Roper made a speciality of hostile accounts of what he conceived of as irrational ideologies, which was no doubt one of the things that drew him to the study of Nazism; but he also went to some lengths to set them in their social and cultural context. As Regius Professor, he conveyed to generations of undergraduates, and not a few postgraduate research students as well, an almost natural assumption not only that history should range across culture, society and belief as well as politics and diplomacy, but also that it should cross national and linguistic boundaries and concern itself with big questions and broad comparative themes. Trevor-Roper's later discomfiture as the authenticator of the spurious Hitler diaries in 1983 could not, in the end, disrupt this vital legacy.

It seemed obvious, indeed, after the war, that History teaching in British schools and universities should include courses on Continental Europe. This created a demand which the wartime generation of historians stepped in to fill. Characteristic was the experience of Michael (later Sir Michael) Howard. Born in 1922, with German relations, and already something of a linguist at Wellington School, Howard began studying European History with Trevor-Roper, A. J. P. Taylor and the French Revolutionary historian J. M. Thompson at Oxford, then, after wartime service in Italy, he returned to complete his degree. Through school connections he landed a job as Lecturer in History at King's College, London, where, since he was replacing a seventeenth-century English specialist, he assumed he was going to teach about seventeenth-century England. After some time, receiving no guidance from the Department, he telephoned a fortnight before term began and was informed that he was 'expected to teach not early-modern English history, but modern European history from 1750 to 1914 and lecture on the subject twice a week'.

While compiling his lectures 'from elderly secondary sources', he cast about for a subject to research. Being a retired army Captain, he was put in charge of a new Department of War Studies at the College, largely the creation of Sir Charles Webster, who told him he had to write a book ('"Not just a few bloody articles", he insisted, "a proper book"'). Clearly it had to be about a war. The least-known and most manageable of modern wars seemed to be the Franco-Prussian War of 1870–1. Howard found a treasure-trove of contemporary and near-contemporary books and pamphlets on the topic about to be thrown out of the library of the Royal United Services Institute. He acquired them for the nucleus of the War Studies Department library at King's, and the basis for his book, which became a classic and is still in print today. It has, however, never been translated into French or German. 'Perhaps', he speculates, 'the France of De Gaulle's Fifth Republic did not want to be reminded by an Englishman of its humiliations, while the Germany of Konrad Adenauer's Federal Republic was as unwilling to recall its military triumphs as were the French their military disasters.'

From his position at King's, and later at Oxford as Regius Professor, Howard trained up more than one generation of military historians, many of whom worked on the history of warfare in Continental Europe. Despite the elements of chance and happenstance in his early career, entertainingly recounted in his beguiling autobiography *Captain Professor* (2006), Howard was in fact part of a broader phenomenon of British historians whose experience in wartime aroused in them a serious interest in the European past. If we want to know how and why the British interest in Continental history developed in the twentieth century, it is indeed important to remember, as Sir Ian Kershaw points out,

> the fact that Britain has been centrally involved in both the World Wars, and that some prominent historians (Trevor-Roper, Bullock, D. C. Watt, Michael Howard, James Joll, M. R. D. Foot, Bill Carr, Wheeler-Bennett, E. H. Carr, to name a few) served in the war or in significant government positions, or both, then brought experience as well as 'engagement' to bear in their university teaching, inspiring, as did some émigré historians, an interest among their students in the history of parts of a troubled Continent.

These historians included, as Kershaw mentions, William Carr (1921–91), author of studies of the unification of Germany and on Nazi foreign policy, who came to his subject as a result of service in the army, including the forces occupying Schleswig-Holstein, which became the topic of his first book; the diplomatic historian Donald Cameron Watt; the intellectual and cultural historian James Joll; and the historian of the British Special Operations Executive Michael (M. R. D.) Foot – all of whom occupied senior positions in British universities from the 1950s to the 1980s. There were many more. Some, like Denys Hay (1915–94) or Sir John Hale (1923–99), devoted themselves to the cultural history of the Italian Renaissance, though the latter only found his subject after an early pre-occupation with the Emperor Napoleon. Most studied more recent history. British university History Departments in the 1960s and 1970s had a stronger presence of European historians than ever before, often exerting a strong fascination over impressionable undergraduates.

VII

Somewhat aside from all this, the French Revolution and Napoleonic period continued to preoccupy a number of British historians throughout the twentieth century. John Holland Rose (1855–1942), who taught at Cambridge, published a widely read biography of Napoleon, while his counterpart in Oxford, James (J. M.) Thompson (1878–1956), produced a string of textbooks which established themselves as the standard works on the French Revolution in the interwar period and for some time afterwards. Both men sought to achieve some kind of balanced interpretation, though at bottom they were Francophiles whose principal role was to make French research on the Revolutionary and Napoleonic eras accessible to an English student readership.

Thompson, for example, saw the Revolution fundamentally as an attempt to create a just, free and rationally ordered society, and to escape from the lack of liberty which he thought characterized the *ancien régime*. A clergyman himself, he had moved before the First World War from High Anglicanism to a rationalist position from which he derided such beliefs as the Virgin Birth as mere superstitions, and had narrowly escaped being removed from his position as a tutor in Divinity at Magdalen College, Oxford. His enthusiasm for France was kindled by service in the Red Cross on the Western Front, and when he returned to Magdalen after the war, it was in the safer position of Tutor in Modern History. In a younger generation, Alfred Cobban (1901–68) broke new ground with his determinedly analytical and sceptical approach to the Revolution; at the height of the Cold War he created a storm with a ferocious attack on the then-dominant Marxist interpretations of Georges Lefebvre and other leading French specialists, *The Social Interpretation of the French Revolution* (1971), but he was also a gifted writer of narrative, whose *Penguin History of Modern France* was widely read by more than one generation of students.

In Cambridge, French history was taught during the postwar decades mainly by Patrick (J. P. T.) Bury (1908–87), nephew of the Regius Professor of Modern History in the early part of the twentieth century. Patrick Bury's early career followed a familiar pattern amongst the diplomatic historians of the interwar years, with ten volumes of *Documents on British Foreign Policy 1919–1939* edited after the end of the Second World War, and work in the Foreign Office Research Department during the war itself, in the French and Low Countries section. But his principal interest was in nineteenth-century French history. As an undergraduate, he won a scholarship to carry out a small research project in Paris and, under the terms of the scholarship, met a number of eminent French historians and intellectuals. This got him interested in the history of the French Third Republic. He embarked on a trilogy on the nineteenth-century French politician Léon Gambetta, publishing the first volume in 1936, and the final volume as late as 1982. These were remarkable for their extensive knowledge of primary sources, unusual amongst British historians of France at the time. During the war, Bury became friendly with a number of the Free French, led by Charles de Gaulle, and his personal contacts and experiences lent his textbook *France 1814–1940*, published in 1949, an authority that saw it through numerous editions; indeed, it is still in print today. Towards the end of his career, he wrote, with Robert Tombs, an important biography of another great nineteenth-century French politician, Adolphe Thiers (1986). His focus on biography was unusual, perhaps; but in his combination of government service and personal experience he falls squarely into the more general pattern of British historians of Europe in the first half of the twentieth century.

For up to the 1960s, all these historians – and there were others, including David Thomson, author of a penetrating if somewhat schematic analysis of democracy in modern French history, and Sir Denis Brogan, whose detailed narrative history of modern France was plundered by generations of students in search of material for their essays – were essentially continuing the tradition established in the second half of the nineteenth century of using printed documents and secondary studies rather than producing works of original research; Bury was an exception here. But the mould was decisively broken by the extraordinary figure of Richard Cobb, whose influence on the study of European history in Britain can, in retrospect, scarcely be overestimated. Richard Cobb was born in 1917, and by the time of his death in 1996 he had become one of the world's leading historians of France, as well known in the country he studied as he was in the country where he was born. He claimed to have become interested in French History quite by accident. When, in December 1934, he was awarded a scholarship to read Modern History at Oxford, his school (Shrewsbury) heaved a sigh of relief and told him not to return. It would be better, indeed, his headmaster told Cobb's mother, if the young man spent the rest of the academic year out of the country altogether. It is not certain what crimes he had committed at the school, but his parents took the hint and sent him to Austria. Here, looking for contacts in an alien environment, he visited the offices of the Society of Friends, the Quakers, where an American lady Quaker involved him in support activities for Social Democrats imprisoned after the brief but violent civil war of February 1934. When he tried to distribute some leaflets, he was arrested and beaten up by the police; they gave him the choice of either reporting to them at nine every morning or leaving the country within twenty-four hours – wisely, perhaps, he chose the latter course of action, and took a train to Strasbourg. By the end of January 1935 he was in Paris, lodging with a family friend. Since he was supposed to be studying History, and had nothing better to do, he began to go to libraries to read about the French Revolution, the only aspect of French history he had heard about. Soon, his awakening interest had become an obsession.

By the time he had to leave for Oxford, Cobb was reading and speaking French fluently, and he had become a passionate partisan of Robespierre and the Revolutionaries of 1789. He now returned to Paris at every opportunity. He was acquiring what he later called 'a second identity, a crossing of the line that is the most important requisite for the English specialist of the history and culture of a foreign society'. His reading on the French Revolution led to the Sorbonne lectures of Georges Lefebvre, the leading historian of the French Revolution. After graduating from Oxford in 1938, Cobb returned to Paris to begin doctoral research under Lefebvre, on the far-left group of the Hébertistes in the early 1790s, but the war interrupted his studies. By chance he was in England when France was overrun by the German army in 1940. He served in the British army as a storeman, and returned to France in 1944 with the invading Allied forces. By 1946 he was demobilized and back in Paris, living nominally on the Left Bank but, he wrote later, often 'waking up in the morning in unknown rooms and trying to guess, from the quality of the light and from the sounds of the street, in which quarter I had landed up on the previous evening'. He returned to teaching English, and was appointed official English Language teacher at the École Nationale Agronomique, a salaried post that was required by the school's statutes but for which Cobb never had any students; he was paid monthly in cash for this sinecure for nearly nine years. Prompted by his friend and fellow-historian of the French Revolution Albert Soboul, he also joined the Communist Party – which supplied him with free evening meals – signing petitions and writing newspaper articles opposing German rearmament.

Back in the archives, he discovered after some months of working through the files that the subject of the Hébertistes was not a suitable one for a dissertation: the group scarcely existed in reality, as Soboul, working through the same material, had also realized. Soboul took up the study of the Parisian Revolutionary Sections of the *sans-culottes* instead, while Cobb stumbled upon records of the marauding bands of *sans-culottes* who were sent out to requisition grain and foodstuffs from the land to feed the starving townspeople, the so-called *Armées Révolutionnaires*. Cobb decided to research not just the Parisian *Armée* but all fifty of them, which took him to provincial archives all over France:

> Once he had found his subject [Cobb later wrote], Soboul
> worked with speed and determination, to a careful plan
> and with a vigorous refusal to allow himself to be led
> down any side channels. My own method – this is perhaps
> not the right word – was very different. I was in no hurry
> – I was not aiming at any particular career in England;
> more and more I enjoyed the excitement of research and
> the acquisition of material, often on quite peripheral
> subjects, as ends in themselves. I allowed myself to be
> deflected down unexpected channels . . . I was interested
> in individuals rather than groups; and when I could pin
> down one of them, I naturally wanted to follow him
> through, to pension and grave . . . I researched and wrote
> for my own enjoyment.

Yet Cobb's researches produced one of the few books that claims, as he says at the beginning, to be an exhaustive study of its topic. At 2 volumes and over 1,000 pages, it was a classic French second doctoral thesis – but when he tried to submit it, he discovered that, as he wrote later, 'the administrative process of presenting a thesis for a *Doctorat-ès-lettres* is almost as daunting as that of cremation', so 'after three months of preliminary skirmishing . . . I gave up just beyond the stage at which I had unloaded 150 copies of my main thesis at the *Secrétariat des thèses*. I presume', he added fifteen years later, 'they are still there.'

In 1956, somewhat unexpectedly, he was offered a lectureship at the University of Wales in Aberystwyth, about as far as one could get from Bohemian life in Paris; after toying with the idea of going to Paris once a month to collect his salary from the agricultural school, he thought better of it and resigned his position, along with his membership of the Communist Party. He subsequently moved to other academic positions, at Manchester, Leeds and finally Oxford. By this time he was married – to an Englishwoman – and had a family. He began to acquire another identity – as an Oxford eccentric, recreating something of the atmosphere of proletarian Paris street life in the quadrangles of Balliol College, where he could often be heard in the late hours, after his third or fourth bottle of wine, haranguing passers-by in Parisian argot.

Yet whatever the excesses of the night before, Cobb was always at his desk the following morning. In Oxford he wrote a series of books, for the first time in English, on aspects of the French Revolution, partly based on his old notes, partly on new research, though he did less and less of this as time went on. The more distant he became from his period of being a Frenchman in the 1930s, 1940s and early 1950s, the stronger became the autobiographical element in his work. 'The writing of history is a form of involvement', he later wrote. History was bound up with experience: 'Since 1935', he said some three decades later, 'I have walked French popular history, drunk it, seen it, heard it, participated in it, walking hand in hand with fraternity and liberty, both first discovered by me in Paris, I have been deeply involved in every event affecting the French people during the last thirty-two years, I make no claim to impartiality, for I am inside not outside my subject; I have acquired a new nationality.'

At the same time, Cobb believed that having shared the experiences of the French people, having come to know them from the inside out, he was entitled to add to the sources from his own fund of experience and knowledge where this was necessary. He freely used the popular literature of the epoch he was writing about – but, he added, where such sources were not sufficient to 'give movement to names, warmth and animation to provincial or professional groups', he had 'not been afraid to fall back on my own imagination and do some of the thinking of the *petit peuple* for them. A certain amount of guesswork and imaginative reconstruction', he added, 'is indispensable, especially in a field so under-represented as popular history'. 'Perhaps', he confessed nervously, 'I have taken too many liberties.' But his experience meant that he was entitled to, he believed. In all his books, Cobb stayed close to his sources, regarding them with a fascination bordering on fetishism. In *The Police and the People*, there are 55 pages of notes containing lengthy extracts from the sources, each of which often extends to half a page or more, for 324 pages of text. *Reactions to the French Revolution* has 80 pages of these notes for 211 pages of text. *Paris and its Provinces* had 40 pages of notes of a similar kind, for 213 pages of text (perhaps the hand of an editor at Oxford University Press had been at work here). The extracts, in the original French, convey a strong flavour of the period, and give practical expression to Cobb's belief that the historian should, where possible, let the people of the past speak for themselves.

What he presented in his studies of the history of the poor, the dispossessed and the destitute in the French Revolution was superficially similar to the studies of the popular movement begun at the same time by other historians after the Second World War, under Lefebvre's supervision. One of Cobb's fellow researchers was George Rudé (1910–93), whose studies of the crowd in the French Revolution pioneered 'history from below'. Rudé was in fact half-Norwegian, spent much of his childhood in Norway, and came to French history through the study of Modern Languages at Cambridge. He became a fully paid-up member of the Communist Party after a visit to the Soviet Union; his political activities made it virtually impossible to get a university post in Britain, and, after a period as a schoolteacher, he obtained a post in Australia, where the suspicious authorities kept him under close surveillance. Subsequently he moved to George Williams University in Canada. None of this, however, prevented his books and articles from exercising a strong methodological influence on younger historians. Another of Cobb's contemporaries was Norman Hampson, who had found his subject – the navy in the French Revolution – as a result of acting as a naval liaison officer with the Free French during the war.

All three lived for long stretches of time in Paris, all of them were members of, or close to, the Communist Party, and all of them subscribed implicitly or explicitly to Lefebvre's Marxist interpretation of the Revolution as the outcome of class struggle. While Soboul and Rudé found order amongst the *sans-culottes* and their spectacular crowd actions, however, Cobb found only disorder in his marauding bands. While the others analysed and categorized their subjects in terms of the nascent class structures of emerging capitalism, Cobb celebrated their individuality. 'I have . . . endeavoured to . . . mark the pitfalls, ravines, and swamps of popular history, particular in its comparative study', he remarked in the Introduction to *The Police and the People*: '"So-and-so, who attempted to write an Anatomy of Revolution, disappeared here without a trace." At least', he added, 'no one is likely to accuse me of writing history that is either comparative or "scientific", or of seeking to establish general laws.' At every point, therefore, he sought to undermine the generalizations of the Marxists. Rudé's carefully compiled social analysis of the rioters was, said Cobb, misleading because those arrested – whose police files provided the basis for Rudé's work – were representative not of the crowd but of the police's assumptions about who was guilty. It was not surprising that the leader in a riot often seemed to be riding on a white horse because anybody riding on a white horse would be assumed by the police to be the leader. The police needed evidence of success, and they were none too scrupulous about how they got it. At its most fundamental, writing history in order to analyse and categorize did serious violence to the people of the past. 'It is possible', Cobb conceded, 'to write history that is in no way human.' But in the end, history was 'not a science . . . The writing of history is one of the fullest and most rewarding expressions of an individual personality.' The historian's 'principal aim is to make the dead live'.

The historian, he wrote, was 'a stationary witness, an observer of a swirling collectivity of which he is not a part'. Like an old man on a street corner, or a lone drinker in a pavement café, the historian too was 'lonely, given to fantasy, having to make do with a few scraps of evidence, in an effort to give life to the passing faces'. Or he was like the Commissaire Maigret, Georges Simenon's detective hero, whose ability to solve crimes depended on his intimate knowledge of the environment in which they were committed: a man who can piece together 'a life, a pattern of work and leisure . . . from a few scraps of evidence'; only an intimate acquaintance with the contest from which these scraps came, an acquaintance born of experience, can make such reconstruction possible. Cobb thus believed it was impossible 'to divorce history from experience'. He wrote history, as he freely admitted, 'subjectively'. His books became increasingly episodic, and steadily less obviously connected with the subject-matter that their titles led the unwary reader to expect.

If *The Police and the People* still has some coherence as a study of protest and order during the Revolution and after, *Reactions to the French Revolution* presents a mixed bag of provincial terrorists and counter-revolutionaries, leading on to an examination of the lives of the poor and the deviant, to which, it argues, the Revolution was largely irrelevant. *Paris and its Provinces* deals with a colourful variety of characters, from bandits and smugglers to millers and horse-thieves – there are reflections on how individuals coped with moving from Paris to the surrounding countryside, and the role of rivers and woods in governing the routes people took, but there is little or no institutional history involved, and by this stage in Cobb's writing career, he has become suspicious of almost any generalizations: 'I do not really know what many Parisians thought about the Versaillais', he writes, in a chapter on the relationship of Paris to Versailles, 'but I do know that one Parisian at least described them as a population of lackeys.' Even with the individual there are mysteries: 'The task of the historian, especially if he is a specialist of social history, is very much akin to that of a novelist. There must be a wide element of guesswork. It is like attempting to sound the unsoundable and to penetrate the secrets of the human heart.' By the time of his next book, *Death in Paris*, Cobb is attempting no more than an explanation of a long series of individual cases of suicide, using the geographical context to explain their actions, insofar as they can be explained at all.

The merging of history and autobiography in his work became increasingly obvious, as the introductions to his books grew ever more autobiographical, and ever more tenuously connected with the books' subject-matter. 'I have been unable', he confessed, 'to separate my own identity from what I have written.' It was scarcely surprising, therefore, that he gradually began to abandon the history of the French Revolution altogether and write about himself instead; after some collections of essays, a book on *The Streets of Paris* (1980), and another, drawing on the memories of his friends in France and Belgium, entitled *French and Germans, Germans and French: A Personal Interpretation of France under Two Occupations, 1914–1918/1940–44* (1983), he turned to writing about his childhood in *Still Life: Sketches from a Tunbridge Wells Childhood* (1984), *A Classical Education* (1985) and *Something to Hold Onto* (1988). Here his almost photographic memory and his extraordinary feel for places and moments are given full rein; but also, too, is his imagination, so that in *A Classical Education*, for example, a tale of his friendship with a young murderer, it is impossible to tell what is fact and what is fiction. Maybe Cobb could no longer tell either; indeed maybe he had long ceased to be able to tell the difference – *Death in Paris*, for example, was severely criticized for its inaccuracy despite its claim to be closely based on police documentation.

Moreover, the confusion of identities in almost all of Cobb's work, and certainly in his English-language books, meant that even his more strictly historical work was also in a sense autobiographical, for he remade the common people of the French Revolution in his own self-image: disorderly, untameable, anarchic, unclassifiable. He avoided writing about the rich and the powerful, the fanatical and the ideological, because he was none of these things himself. More profoundly, perhaps, his confession that he felt lonely and isolated in France, looking at the French people going by on the street or wandering through the pages of the documents he read, might be understood as an unconscious confession that he too, in the end, remained an outsider: an Englishman who might have spoken French with an accent and inflexion indistinguish-able from that of the ordinary working-class Parisian, but an Englishman none the less, looking at the French from the outside. In the last chapter of *The End of the Line*, written just two days before his death in 1996, Cobb insisted: 'I am not a novelist and could not rise to literary invention. My characters, those who figure in my social observation, are *real*, and not just forms of self-congratulatory indulgence within the context of food or drink.' But the fact that he felt it necessary to make this declaration suggests, I think, an element of doubt. Perhaps the best verdict on his work was passed by Raymond Carr, who described one of his books as 'a work of genius; but the work of a poet as much as of a historian'. In this respect, though he would probably have hated the comparison, he was not unlike Thomas Carlyle, whose reliance on intuition and imagination was just as great if not more so, though it was an imagination, unlike Cobb's, thoroughly divorced from experience.

Cobb's reputation meant that he also quickly built up a large school of brilliant doctoral students, almost all of whom researched aspects of provincial French history in the early 1790s, and many of whom, like Colin Lucas, Alan

Forrest, Gwynne Lewis, Martyn Lyons, James F. McMillan or Colin Jones, went on to become leading historians of their generation. Their collective achievement, along with Cobb, was perhaps threefold: first, to reorient the French Revolution away from Paris and towards the provinces, to show it as a more widespread and varied phenomenon than conventionally understood; second, again along with Cobb in his English-language works, to uncover the neglected history of the Directory, between the fall of Robespierre in 1794 and the arrival of Napoleon in 1799; and finally, by focusing on the ordinary, often unpolitical poor, especially in the provinces, to cast a sceptical light on patriotic and Marxist narratives of the national uprising of the French lower classes. One way of looking at their work is indeed in the context of the age-old debate, going back at least as far as Carlyle, between the advocates of history as the playground of vast impersonal forces and the champions of history as the operation of individual free will; Cobb did not exactly believe that the will of ordinary people was unfettered by circumstance, such as poverty, hunger and destitution, but in many respects he was indeed an extreme example of the individualizing tendencies of many British historians since the early nineteenth century. The 'second identity' he urged all British historians of the Continent to acquire, whether they worked on France, Germany, Italy, Russia or some other country, held up a seductive vision that many younger historians followed, but in the end it could not prevent Cobb himself, or indeed many of those who imbibed his message, from remaining fundamentally British in their approach to the past.

4

A sense of adventure

I

In the 1950s and especially the 1960s, the landscape of Higher Education in the UK changed dramatically. A report for the government by the economist Lionel Robbins concluded that Britain was falling behind its rivals because the proportion of young Britons who went to university was too low. It recommended that anyone capable of benefiting from university study should be permitted to undertake it. These recommendations were quickly put into effect. The late nineteenth and early twentieth centuries had seen the creation of the so-called 'redbrick universities', situated in the larger provincial cities, especially in the Midlands and the North, such as Manchester, Birmingham, Sheffield, Leeds, Liverpool and Leicester; History Departments in these universities were often dominated by diplomatic and political historians, though Economic History Departments also emerged in them. Following the Robbins report, the so-called 'plate-glass universities' were founded in the 1960s – Sussex, East Anglia, Warwick, Lancaster, Kent, Stirling, Essex and others – and were joined by a number of upgraded polytechnics. Among other things, this meant a vast expansion of the historical profession, as of other academic professions, with jobs at the new universities virtually going begging for Junior Research Fellows of Oxbridge Colleges, successful doctoral students and, in some cases, postgraduates who had barely embarked on their research.

The new universities were in the vast majority of cases determined to break free from what they saw as the stuffy and conservative mould of the redbricks and profile themselves as innovative, pathbreaking institutions. They became the home of the latest trend in History – Social History, located at Warwick in the Centre for Social History, at most other places squarely in the middle of the History Department or as a section within an Interdisciplinary School. Social reform, social change and social movements were on the contemporary agenda in the 1960s, so it was not surprising that Social History should be at the cutting edge. So great was the excess of demand over supply that in any case it would have been difficult to keep social historians out.

Crucially, the traditional division of History Departments into British and European History, replicating the fixed dualism of the A-level examinations at secondary school, was imported into the new universities, though a number expanded it by including other parts of the world as well. A new generation of British Europeanists thus entered university employment. Historians like Carsten and Cobb were encouraging archival research. Foreign travel was rapidly becoming easier and cheaper. New grants for research were becoming available. The perceived need to encourage friendship and co-operation between young people of different European nations and overcome the legacy of hatred left by two World Wars had led to the endowment of a number of government grants for foreign study, international exchange agreements, and scholarships for foreign students.

The teaching and learning of European languages was still widespread in academic secondary education in Britain. And in the 1970s, Britain's entry into the European Community, as it then was, created further opportunities, as well as a sense of commitment amongst thinking young people to the European ideal. The economic boom of the postwar years stood in strong contrast to the catastrophic economic condition of Europe between the wars. This intensification of contacts between British and Continental historians reflected in part a growing political and ideological convergence. The Cold War was beginning to thaw. Franco died. It would not have been possible in the interwar years, when Fascism, Communism and National Socialism created an intellectual gulf that would have been hard to bridge even had authoritarian and totalitarian regimes on the Continent not made contacts difficult in themselves or expelled so many historians from their own countries. Democratic polities made exchanges easier on a number of levels.

All of this encouraged my own generation of British research students to go abroad to do our PhDs. There was a sense that jobs were easier to find in the new universities if you did not work on British history. And because senior positions in British universities, particularly in those that produced large numbers of History PhDs, such as Oxford, Cambridge and London, were now filled to a far greater degree than before by exiled historians who had come over during or before the war, or British historians who had become interested in the Continent through their own personal involvement in one country or another during the conflict, it was far from difficult to find someone to supervise one's work.

Moreover, an older generation of British historians versed in European history and languages from their interwar pursuit of diplomatic history, men such as A. J. P. Taylor and E. H. Carr, also stood ready to help.

And then there was the encouragement offered by a new generation of European history specialists born in the 1930s. Some of these were voluntary expatriates, such as Volker Berghahn or Hartmut Pogge-von Strandmann, or had close personal connections with the Continent, like John Röhl. Historians like Anthony Nicholls published books that for the first time took advantage of the new historical scholarship emerging in the countries they were studying. Tim Mason, born in 1940, and a committed Marxist who made it his life's work to recreate and analyse the German working class's many forms of resistance to Nazism, was an inspirational figure, spending much of his time in Germany, hobnobbing with German Marxists, and publishing most of what he wrote in German rather than English. The end of the Franco regime in Spain in the mid-1970s removed major obstacles to the study of modern Spanish history. The Cold War made funds and training available for those who wished to specialize in Russia or other Eastern European countries, and détente spawned academic exchanges, though archival research was still barely possible. And new institutional structures emerged to foster international exchanges, most notably the West and East European Studies Centres at St Antony's College, Oxford, with its numerous endowed scholarships and visiting professorships, founded shortly after the Second World War, and the German Historical Institute in London, established in the mid-1970s, which brought young German historians to Britain and acted as a centre for British historians working on Germany.

A whole new generation of British historians of Europe thus emerged to occupy university teaching posts in the 1960s and early 1970s, a generation now, in the early twenty-first century, reaching retirement age: the product of a historically unique intersection of the baby-boomers, who came of age during this period, with the large cohort of more senior historians of Europe that had emerged in or immediately after the Second World War. This, in essence, was the conjuncture that created the British European History tradition in the second half of the twentieth century. At the same time, there was also a wider and more varied set of impulses that brought the baby-boomers and their successors to an interest in European History. These naturally varied according to which country they chose to study, and, in doing so, connected with much older, more deeply rooted traditions of British interest in the Continent.

II

For the postwar generation, the baby-boomers, Germany exerted a powerful fascination. Born in 1947, for instance, I grew up in the suburbs of London, near the East End, and often saw bomb-sites when we went shopping in Leytonstone or Walthamstow, with houses missing from terraced rows like gaps in a row of teeth, the wallpaper and fireplaces in their bedrooms exposed in shocking intimacy. I played with the gas-masks in my great-aunt's air-raid shelter in Ilford, and listened to my parents and their friends reminiscing about the war. My mother frequently took me to see war films like *Reach for the Sky* and *Battle of the River Plate*, I read comics full of war stories, and played 'Tommies and Jerries' in the garden with the boys next door. In 1965 I felt moved to go with some schoolfriends to Winston Churchill's funeral, which seemed in some indefinable way to mark the end of the postwar era and draw a line under the wartime experience. I stood on Ludgate Hill as grand wartime figures walked or drove by, all now (or so it seemed to me) extremely aged and about to pass from the scene. Memories of the war pervaded my childhood, and with them, of course, Germany and the Germans were an ever-present remembered menace. Far more than any other European country, Germany was a major factor in the culture in which my generation was brought up. 'I never had to decide when to work on German rather than British history', writes Tim Blanning, born in 1942, 'since I have been obsessed with all things German for as long as I can remember. This was certainly well under way by the time I reached prep school aged 8.'

More generally, the new opportunities for travel on the Continent in the 1950s came together with schoolteachers' discovery of Europe during the Second World War to encourage an interest in European History in the younger generation. 'I'm sure', writes Norman Davies, who grew up in the North of England but as a child stubbornly identified himself with his Welsh ancestry, 'there never was a time when I was more attracted to British/English history than to continental history.' His interest was aroused at school 'by a scoutmaster who took us on a series of continental treks – to Brittany, to Luxembourg, to Austria and to Yugoslavia – and who, as my

Geography teacher, taught me scholarship Geography using French textbooks'. So when he left school, Davies went to France as an early pioneer of the now-commonplace gap year, studying at the University of Grenoble and then organizing with a group of school friends 'an expedition by Willys jeep from Bolton to Istanbul via the Iron Curtain. This', he now thinks, 'was the start of my interest in Eastern Europe.' But at Oxford his interest in things non-British proved a disaster. His tutor A. J. P. Taylor left a lasting intellectual mark on him, teaching him among other things to write with wonderful and often provocative clarity, but his choice of 'The Age of Dante' as his document-based Special Subject required him to spend so much time improving his basic school Italian sufficiently to master the *Divine Comedy* in the original that he was never able to get up to speed with his Modern English History paper: 'my total ignorance on that subject cost me a First. At which point, I decided to become a schoolmaster.'

Davies applied to St Paul's School in London for a job as a History teacher, but they were also interviewing for a French teacher the same day, and a series of confusions in the waiting-room led to his being interviewed for the latter post instead of the former; his effortless command of the language prompted the interviewers to offer him the job 'in front of a field of applicants all of whom had Oxbridge Firsts in Modern Languages'. He had already taught himself Russian, and such was his linguistic facility that when 'the Russian master fell seriously ill, I was told to take on his classes and to go to night school'. But he felt his Russian was not up to scratch. A term at Cambridge taking an intensive Russian course still left him dissatisfied with his progress, so he left schoolteaching and went to Sussex University to do a degree in Russian. By sheer chance, he found himself lodging with a Polish landlord, who, learning of his topic, insisted he take on Polish as well; this proved so challenging and absorbing that when he graduated he went straight to Poland and did not return for three years. While he was there, his old Tutor A. J. P. Taylor urged him to write a book on the Russo-Polish War of 1919–20, since his command of both languages was highly unusual. Davies obliged, registering at Cracow University for a PhD, though under the then Communist regime it was forbidden to write about the topic, so he had to pretend he was writing on British foreign policy towards Poland in the years in question instead. Completed in 1968, the thesis was published in 1972 as *White Eagle, Red Star: The Polish–Soviet War, 1919–20*, by which time he had been appointed as a Lecturer in Polish History at London University's School of Slavonic and East European Studies.

The presence of Continental exiles and expatriates in Britain also played a role in shaping the career choices of a younger generation of historians including, for example, Robert Frost, currently Professor of Early Modern History at Aberdeen University. Determined to be a historian, he had little idea of what he wanted to do for his doctorate when he graduated from St Andrews. Then he

> happened to see an advert for an exchange on a summer school to the Jagiellonian University in Cracow. Links had started in the 70s, partly because of the Polish community in Fife, a legacy of the RAF base at Leuchars in World War II (there is a mural of Polish airmen in St Andrews Town Hall). I had worked all my long vacations, and if

161

the university wanted to pay for me to spend six weeks in Poland, what the hell? Poland, Bulgaria, I didn't care.

His Tutor – Geoffrey Parker, a historian of early modern Europe who specialized in Spain and the Netherlands – had just returned from a trip to Warsaw and advised him to do a PhD on seventeenth-century Poland, an important but almost totally neglected topic. 'The best advice I ever had', recalls Frost, and he fell instantly in love with Poland and its language and culture. He returned on graduating and spent two years learning the language, studying at Cracow University and living through the rise of the Solidarity trade union movement and the subsequent imposition of martial law. On his return he embarked on a PhD at the School of Slavonic and East European Studies in London under the supervision of Norman Davies, publishing it in 1993 as *After the Deluge: Poland-Lithuania and the Second Northern War.*

III

'Why continental history? I never imagined doing anything else', concurs Catherine Merridale. Like at least some others, she saw it as a means of escaping Britain, where she felt 'hemmed in'. In her case, literally so: 'I ran away from home when I was fifteen', she confesses; rejecting any half-measures, she ran all the way to France, and when she came back to resume her schooling, her teachers soon 'moved me out of the French class (disruptive) and offered to teach me German instead. Being awkward by nature', she goes on, 'I decided to ditch that and learn Russian when an unusually dedicated teacher (at a state comp[rehensive school]) offered to teach it to me in her own time.' By the time she got to university (she studied History at Cambridge), she had gathered a good deal of experience on the Continent: 'Europe was my hunting-ground. I'd learned a stack of its languages, hitch-hiked over it, read about it . . . and wanted to know more about it.' For her what mattered was that, in Russian history in particular, 'the questions were big and that was what I needed'. 'I should have realized', she says, looking back, 'that my archives would be a long and expensive journey away for the rest of my life, and also that I'd have years of agony trying to find students who could do research with me (since Russian is not exactly popular in schools)', but in the end, she concludes, 'none of that mattered, and if I'm honest it still doesn't.'

If the influence of exiles and émigrés has played a role in the decision of British historians like Norman Davies and Robert Frost to study the European rather than the British past, then for Catherine Merridale, for all the impact of chance circumstance, a desire for personal and intellectual adventure has been the driving force. It was the same for many others. 'A sense of adventure/intrigue/general nosiness' inspired Tim Cole, who teaches European History at Bristol University. 'I wonder', he muses, 'if as historians we are captured by a fascination with this other world of the past. For those of us who stray away from the UK in our research, this is perhaps a double otherness of both time and space.' A desire 'to learn a new language, live in a new place, invest in trying to under-stand the past of a place other than the UK' led him to Hungary, where he embarked on a study of the social geography of the ghettoization of the Jews in the 1940s and their deportation to Auschwitz. Similarly, David Moon, Professor of History

163

at Durham and author of, among other things, *The Russian Peasantry, 1600–1930: The World the Peasants Made* (1999), 'decided to work on continental European history precisely because I wanted to research the history of a society quite different from my own experiences in Britain. For this reason', he adds, 'I chose Russian rather than western European history.'

Guy Rowlands had a similar experience: 'At secondary school we covered the first half of seventeenth-century Continental Europe for A-levels, and I found it simply more "exotic" than the Tudors and early Stuarts, whom I had studied on repeated occasions since the age of 8.' In rather similar terms, Dame Olwen Hufton, author of numerous books on eighteenth-century France and Europe, confesses that, for her, 'Continental history had an exotic dimension'. Robert Gildea, now Professor of Modern History at Oxford and author of a string of important works on nineteenth- and twentieth-century France, writes that 'even at school I thought that British history was in black and white and European history in technicolour'. Kevin Passmore, who teaches at Cardiff University, visited France on a school exchange scheme at the age of fourteen and became fascinated by its 'otherness'. The same held true of its history: at A-level he already 'found the succession of revolutions and reactions in France far more interesting than the stability of British history'. Active on the political left, he began 'to see France as a model for Britain'. France, indeed, could seem more exciting in the present as well: Robert Tombs, for example, began working on a PhD on the Paris Commune of 1871 in the wake of what many have seen as the last outbreak of revolutionary fever in French history, the student revolts of May 1968.

Sometimes this motivation could derive from childhood enthusiasms. Guy Rowlands was turned on to French history as a child. 'From the age of about 10', he writes, 'I had a strong interest in seventeenth-century Europe, having been captivated by a wonderful children's summer-holiday tv series in the 1970s/early 80s called "The Flashing Blade", dubbed from French, and set in the War of the Mantuan Succession! Toe-curling, I know', he admits; but his experience is far from untypical. Peter Campbell confesses: 'I loved history from the age of 6 when I read Ladybird History books about King Alfred, Boudicca, Charles I', though it was Cobban's *Penguin History of France* that really got him interested in non-British history and the same author's *Aspects of the French Revolution* that kindled his interest in 1789 and its origins, both read when he was at school. My own interest in Germany and the First World War was sparked by, among other things, reading the *Biggles* books by Captain W. E. Johns, of which there was a complete set in my school library. Coming to them when I was ten, I found the early, more realistic stories, set in the world of the Royal Flying Corps in the years 1914–18, horrifying and exciting in equal measure. It was a problem, admittedly, that Biggles never aged, and remained a young man even in later stories set in the 1950s. However, after that, I never stopped reading about history in one form or another. Other historians I know were gripped too, as I was, by reading Rudyard Kipling's *Puck of Pook's Hill*, where the author makes the past come alive as a succession of figures, beginning with a Roman legionary stationed in Britain, emerge from the past thanks to a magic spell, to tell their stories to a group of picnicking children. Such experiences did not necessarily inspire an exclusive interest in European history, but if the book was the right one, it could certainly exert a powerful influence in that direction.

A number of historians who have chosen to specialize in the history of the European Continent have found British history rather dull in comparison. Patrick Major 'always found British history rather tedious – only Mrs Thatcher', he adds, 'seemed to make the present uncomfortably interesting, but I had to live through that. German history always appeared to be overflowing with change. The Germans were sufficiently similar but different to be fascinating' – not least because, at school, he was taught German by an elderly Jewish exile from Hitler's Third Reich, who had personally witnessed the rise of Nazism and often turned German lessons into History lessons – another example of the émigré influence. By the age of sixteen, Peter Jones had 'already come to the conclusion . . . that British history was boring'. For some, the route could begin in Britain and end in France. Ruth Scurr, author of a widely acclaimed biography of Robespierre, began with an interest in the ideas of Adam Smith, which led to a study of the influence on him of French economic thinkers. She 'found that the French Revolution exerts what seems almost to be a magnetic pull on 18th-century historical studies. I became more and more fascinated by what had happened to the socio-economic ideas I'd been mapping once they entered the maelstrom of the Revolution.' In due course, this led her to 'Robespierre, whose policies and beliefs were the polemical target of much of the sophisticated thinking I'd been investigating'.

Medievalists in particular seem to have felt repelled by what R. I. Moore, recently retired from the Chair of Medieval

History at Newcastle University and author of a celebrated book, *The Formation of a Persecuting Society*, published in 1987, calls the 'parochialism' and 'intellectual smugness' of English Medieval History at Oxford during his days as an undergraduate there. 'One of my Tutors', he recalls, 'used to tell the story that when he expressed an interest in working on Spanish history to [the celebrated medievalist] K. B. Macfarlane, he received the reply: "It will be time enough for that when you have made a contribution to the history of your own country." It was not an uncommon attitude.' Rosamond McKitterick found British History simply 'too insular' even at school, while at university she discovered that

> the historiography and themes debated by scholars of Continental history were far more open and less focused on a narrow set of political questions than it seemed to be in the little British history I did ... It was not only insular but seemed to argue about the same political topics with all the paths already charted. There seemed little room for branching out and making new paths.

Relocated to Australia at the age of seven, she encountered a colourful range of immigrants, including Hungarians, Greeks, Italians and many others, at university, and this multicultural diversity aroused her interest. 'While the experience as a whole precipitated me back to England as soon as I could manage it', she says, 'it still did not make me concentrate on English history.' For someone with an interest in medieval history, national boundaries in any case make little sense, and scholarship and debates have a pronounced international flavour. Continental history, for McKitterick, was from the

outset 'exciting, with connections across and between countries, different political and cultural configurations and appar-
ently lots of work to be done'.

Many historians were attracted by what Sir Ian
Kershaw calls 'the drama of Continental history, compared
with the relatively continuous, undramatic course of English/
British history'. Helen Graham confesses that she 'would
never have chosen a British historical specialism', because
of her desire, at the very outset of her career, 'to get to the
bottom of the "dark continental" interwar period' (an allusion to Mark Mazower's history of twentieth-century Europe,
entitled *Dark Continent*). In her case, this quickly became
an 'obsession' with the Spanish Civil War, and with locat-
ing it in a 'comparative European' frame of meaning that
explored 'the origins and development of forms of political
violence that emerged as supposed "solutions" to rapid pro-
cesses of change'. Like others, therefore, she came to her topic
because it seemed to offer better opportunities for answering
large historical questions such as this. 'As an undergraduate',
writes Philip Morgan, who teaches Modern European and
especially Italian History at the University of Hull, '19th- and
20th-century European history just struck me as being more
interesting, or rather, involved me studying more interesting
and significant events.' This attraction has also been exerted
by the way in which Continental history can pose large intellectual challenges that, to many, seem less obvious in British
history. Forced to take a course on French history in the late
seventeenth and early eighteenth centuries at the University
of Lancaster because the teacher of his favoured subject, the
British labour movement, was on leave, Julian Swann found

his new area riven by impassioned debates that raised large and dramatic questions, making for a stark contrast with what he came to consider 'the relative parochialism of British history'. When he discovered the huge and controversial literature on the origins of the French Revolution, he recalls, 'I was hooked', and he has remained so ever since.

In a somewhat similar, if less haphazard manner, Chris Ealham came to his subject 'because I was fascinated by issues like political rupture, revolutionary and protest movements, dictatorship, and so on. As a young man', he adds, 'I'd have preferred to watch paint dry before studying British history.' Lucy Riall 'found in 19th-century Italian history the kinds of questions being asked – about nationalism, state-formation, centre–periphery relations, and social conflict – more interesting than those that I perceived being asked about British or Irish history'. Similarly, David Laven never 'considered working purely on British history. It was simply not a temptation . . . Then and now, the majority of British experts struck me as frighteningly narrow in their approach.' For him, studying Italy, and in particular Venice, seemed a better way into large historical questions about systems of government, or the relationship of centre and periphery. Or, as his sister Mary Laven puts it, British history was all very well, but 'there was a lot of fun to be had elsewhere'.

For those who were interested in the more remote past, such as the medieval period, and began their studies in the 1970s or 1980s, 'the exciting ideas', as Christopher Clark recalls, 'were all coming from continental Europe, or, more precisely, from France – Le Goff, Duby, Le Roy Ladurie . . . and towering over them all were the earlier generations of the

Annales school – Bloch, Febvre, Ariès etc.'. These ideas began to be widely discussed in the English-language literature from the early 1970s onwards, and many of the key works of these historians were translated, finding a readership among British History students who found it difficult to grasp academic French. The *Annales* offered a new way of approaching History that was exciting and seductive. Peter Campbell found British history 'prosaic, dull, steeped in minor debates . . . Now the *Annales* school, that was different, it appealed to the rebel in me as well', since 'the English tradition then [in the 1980s] was a rejection of French ideas'.

The excitement generated by the new French historians was a feeling shared not only by medievalists, as Clark initially intended to become ('I hated modern history and did as little as I possibly could'), and early modernists like Campbell, but by almost anyone interested in new approaches to the study of the past. As a postgraduate in Oxford, studying modern German history, I mixed a lot with other PhD students working with Richard Cobb or Theodore Zeldin on the social history of France, and the excitement they evidently felt about the work of French historians, so utterly different to that of their British counterparts, led me to read books such as Pierre Goubert's *Beauvais et le Beauvaisis*, Le Roy Ladurie's *Les paysans de Languedoc,* François Lebrun's *Les hommes et la mort en Anjou* and Fernand Braudel's *La Méditerranée et le monde Méditerranéen à l'époque de Philippe II*, all of which you could pick up in cheap paperback editions in a wonderful foreign-language bookshop in Oxford. The breadth of these books' conception of history was simply revelatory: anything was grist to the historian's mill, from emotions like fear (the subject of another major book, by Jean Delumeau) to the effects of climate on everyday life. At their best, they succeeded in recapturing the textures of living and experience of ordinary people in utterly remote times and places and bringing them vividly to life.

More exciting still, if possible, was their determination to link together different aspects of past society, showing the relationship between economy, demography, life and death, sickness and health, emotion and experience, social attitudes and antagonisms, and political life, all in one huge, closely interwoven picture, painted on a local or regional canvas, to be sure, but within its confines conveying a total history of every aspect of human existence. They tackled long periods too, the famous *longue durée* of the *Annales* school, and showed the relationship between deeply embedded social and economic structures and short-term, sometimes cataclysmic, events like poor harvests or devastating wars – another central theme of the *Annales*, the relationship between *structure* and *conjuncture*. Later on, without fully realizing it in any conscious sense, I came to apply all of these concepts and ideas to a study of the north German city of Hamburg in the nineteenth century, in which I used a catastrophic cholera epidemic that occurred in 1892 to look at long-term features of the city's economic, social and political life and tease out how they interacted with the disaster, as it were, to shake up the kaleidoscope into a new pattern.

All of this was enormously important, therefore, and not just for medievalists; and yet there were similar influences at work in British History too, which in my case, and no doubt in others too, meshed with the example of the *Annales* school in France in interesting and exciting ways. The 'history work-shops' founded by Raphael Samuel at Ruskin College, Oxford, generated an enormous sense of intellectual excitement and political commitment. Here too there was an attempt to marry the study of larger historical structures with the recreation of immediate lived experience and individual lives in a heady mix that convinced many of us that History was politically impor-tant as well as intellectually satisfying. Much of this work was local in focus, but this did not necessarily make it narrow, any more than the regional focus of the *Annales* historians made theirs narrow. Moreover, however much British historians of the European Continent choose their topic in order to be able to answer big questions, the British tradition of empirically based historical scholarship is also well represented in their own writing and research; indeed, paradoxically perhaps, that is often part of its appeal in countries whose approach is more abstract and theoretical. Perhaps reaching the decision that British history was boring was a necessary step in psyching themselves up to take the risky and arduous trip across the Channel. At the time they took it, they were all in their twen-ties, with only a patchy knowledge of British history and its debates; in the present they would probably recognize how partial their view really was.

IV

The fact that British history has often been taught at school and university in survey courses covering long stretches of time contrasted unfavourably for some with the teaching of European history, which has often involved a wide variety of

topics related to each other in less obvious, perhaps more challenging ways. Or, as Leif Jerram, who teaches at Manchester
University and is the author of a study of urban planning and
design in Weimar Germany, puts it: 'English history was a
game of catch; but "foreign" history was juggling.' For others,
however, the lack of continuities in the subject-matter of
European history as it is taught in the schools is not a challenge
but a problem: David Abulafia, Professor of Mediterranean
History at Cambridge, considers that the 'piecemeal nature of
school courses' means that students 'have no idea of the big
themes and continuities in European history. I think', he adds,
'this is doing enormous damage.'

Inspirational teaching has enthused some with a
desire to study European history – even, in a number of cases,
provided them with a research topic. Guy Rowlands was
drawn to France in particular by his Oxford Tutor, Lawrence
Brockliss, who taught a course on 'Society and Government
in France 1600–1715' and made this seemingly rather dry topic
fascinating by being 'wilfully provocative'. Initially destined
for the army, Rowlands quit the officer school at Sandhurst
when 'within a short space of time I realized how much I was
missing History'; but his military interest did not entirely
desert him, and when he returned to Oxford it was to research
for a doctorate on the French army in the seventeenth century.
Alex Bamji, who recently completed a Cambridge PhD on religion and medicine in early modern Venice and now teaches at
the University of Leeds, considers the most significant influence in bringing her to her topic was 'inspirational teaching
as an undergraduate' by a range of Cambridge historians,
especially Peter Burke, Mary Laven, Melissa Calaresu, and

Ulinka Rublack, who deepened into commitment an interest in European history already awakened at school.

Another recent PhD, Victoria Harris, now a Junior Research Fellow at King's College, Cambridge, though British, took her undergraduate degree at Brown University, Rhode Island, where

> there was this new, hotshot professor at Brown [it was the charismatic Omer Bartov, whose specialism was in fact the German army in the Second World War] teaching a course on the long nineteenth century in Germany. And ultimately the freedom of Brown's curriculum meant that it didn't matter if I strolled in, listened for a few weeks and hated it. So off I went. And it was just fantastic, so I took another one (20th century). And that was that really.

Jill Stephenson, who established her reputation with a pioneering study of women in Nazi Germany, also came to her subject as a result of inspirational teaching, in her case at the University of Edinburgh, where she later spent her career teaching Modern European History:

> I took Arthur Marwick's Special Subject, 'The War and the Welfare State in Britain, 1939–45', and was fascinated by it. That stimulated my interest in social history. But it was my other final year tutor, [the diplomatic historian] Esmonde Robertson, who steered me into German history. Having asked what I wanted to do after my degree and been told that I'd like to do research, he said 'What had you thought of doing?'. So I said 'I've been reading a bit about Lenin recently' – it was all I

could think of. So he said, 'Why don't you do women in Germany between the wars. Germans haven't got round to social history – too preoccupied with war guilt.' So that was it. His wife was a von Lossow and they spent their summers in Ammerland. So he sent me to the IfZ [Institut für Zeitgeschichte, the Institute for Contemporary History, in Munich].

In a rather different way, Robert Gildea, as an Oxford undergraduate, became fascinated by the seminars run by Richard Cobb and Theodore Zeldin, both of whom attracted large numbers of gifted PhD students and generated a real sense that they were engaged in collective projects of innovation, though in very different ways from one another. 'I saw myself', writes Gildea, 'following in their footsteps.'

For some, inspirational teaching had already left its mark at school. Peter Jones, for example, 'was introduced to the French Revolution by an inspirational history teacher' at Wyggeston Boys' Grammar School, which he attended in Leicester. Alison Rowlands studied sixteenth- and seventeenth-century Europe for A-level 'with two inspiring school-teachers'. For others, the conventional division of A-level History into a British and a European topic could have an impact of itself, irrespective of the quality of the teaching. 'My A-level', writes Leif Jerram,

> was divided into two halves: 'Britain, 1685–1914' and 'Revolution and Directory in France'. One half was clearly intended to imbue a broad chronology, and the other – more document-based – was clearly meant to offer depth and critical analysis. I had a fantastic teacher for the

British half who, stodgy and superficial as the subject was, managed to keep it alive. I had a dreadful teacher for the French Revolution half who, despite her best endeavours, could not kill it.

What fascinated him above all was the encounter with original documents – 'Gillray cartoons and *cahiers de doléances*, tax returns and Roman republican symbolism'. Thus already, at school, the syllabus had the effect that 'I never had the faintest idea that the histories of other cultures could be any less important, or useful, or challenging, or fascinating, than those of my own.'

V

The taste for adventure, the search for big ideas, the desire for the exotic or the influence of inspirational teachers, are some of the factors that drove British historians to choose to study the European past. Others came to Continental history through a love of languages. 'With me (as, I suspect, with a good many others in our line of country)', writes Robert Evans, 'the languages came first. So I worked on areas that interested me linguistically.' This turned out above all to be Central Europe, whose languages, including Czech, German, Hungarian, Italian and others, he soon mastered. For some, this could be a rather pragmatic choice. 'I decided on European history rather than British', says Tim Kirk, Professor of European History at Newcastle University and author of a number of books on Austria and Germany under the Nazis, 'because my background was in modern languages – so not so much a choice between Germany or Britain as between history and linguistics.' Others came from languages to history by a rather more roundabout route. Sir Ian Kershaw, who had begun his career working on English medieval history, was dissatisfied with only knowing French and Latin, and started learning German in 1969 through evening classes. German history was just opening up at the time, and the classes had a heavy dose of recent history and politics which led him to take an intensive language course in Germany in 1972 and switch fields to start working on German history.

A love of literature, or a fascination with politics, has been particularly influential as a stimulus in the case of historians of Russia, above all back in the days of the Cold War. 'In the late 1950s', writes Geoffrey Hosking, 'Russia/the Soviet Union seemed a fascinating country':

> It was recovering from Stalinism, it had just launched the first space satellite, and it was widely reputed (then) to be ahead of the west in some fields of science and technology. Its ideology looked at that time in some ways attractive, though it was clear that it had led to appalling evils: finding out why was a fascinating intellectual challenge. On top of that was the appeal of Russian culture, above all the novelists; Pasternak's *Doctor Zhivago* had just appeared, and it suggested that the great tradition was not dead. So I came to Russia, its language and culture, before I became a historian. British history was never a possibility as a career for me.

His path to Russian history was similar to that taken by Edward Acton, who 'fell in love with Alexander Herzen as an undergraduate. In part', he writes, 'I was attracted by his personal philosophy . . . Herzen happened to be a Russian. As an undergraduate I knew no Russian. I was determined to do my doctorate on him and learned Russian at Cambridge for that.' Such influences have also affected younger historians such as Miriam Dobson. Beginning with an interest in Russian literature, she became fascinated by Russian politics during a school trip to Moscow and St Petersburg, and took a degree in Modern Languages with a particular focus on Russian. It was only 'gradually', she says, that her 'interest in contemporary Russia became an interest in the country's history'.

But there were more practical influences at work too. For some, British History seemed an overcrowded field in which getting a job would be more difficult than in other areas. This seems to have been a consideration in virtually every decade. David Laven started researching Italian history

> in part because I thought there would probably be no academic job at the end of my PhD – there were very few in the late 1980s. On account of this I decided to concentrate on a place with which I had a powerful emotional attachment, and a host of friends – a nice environment before I failed to get into the diplomatic service (luckily things had changed by 1990).

Around the same time, Alison Rowlands was advised by her university teachers that she 'should do German history, as I'd have a better chance of a job'. A decade or so earlier, things seemed similar to Robert Frost, who concluded that 'starting a PhD in 1980 was not a good career move, with Margaret Thatcher laying waste to the universities', so living in Poland and learning the language might, he thought, 'lead on to other things, such as journalism or the Foreign

Office'. After two years, fortunately for historical scholarship, he changed his mind, but the seeds of his preoccupation with a Continental country had been sown anyway. David Welch, Professor of Modern History at the University of Kent, 'decided to write on German history because it coincided with Great Britain joining the European Community and I was advised that there would be lashings of funding'. So he abandoned his plans to write a PhD at Berkeley on the Black Panther movement and went to Oxford instead, where, under James Joll's supervision, he wrote a thesis on propaganda and the German cinema in the Third Reich, subsequently published by Oxford University Press. 'When it came to thinking about a possible research topic', Sir John Elliott was 'influenced by the fact that there seemed to be standing room only in British history (already in 1952!)'.

Family influences have proved important for some. Robert Gildea's father, for example, was a British civil servant who played a part in negotiating Britain's entry into the European Union. A convinced European, he believed his children should know about Continental Europe and sent his son on an exchange to France when he was fourteen. David Laven's 'father had fallen in love with Venice in 1945, and ultimately spent much of his life working on Venetian history. In consequence', he adds, 'I spent a lot of time there, and developed a profound affection for the city and its inhabitants.' His sister Mary Laven was (obviously) exposed to the same influences. Thus for her, working on Italian history 'was not an especially brave or adventurous decision'. John Pollard is 'Italian on my mother's side (though sadly she couldn't speak Italian)' and thus felt predisposed towards the history of the European Continent. Similarly, Robert Mallett

> decided to work principally on Italian Fascism because
> I have family roots in north east Italy. My childhood
> was filled with tales of the regime, Mussolini's visit to
> the area, the experience of the Second World War, Nazi
> occupation, the resistance and Allied liberation. To me
> this seemed such an interesting and indeed dark history
> that I was immediately drawn to it, and many years later
> I still find it as fascinating and fundamentally interesting
> as ever.

David Abulafia came to Spanish history not least because of the distant roots of his own family in the country, 'though as it happens', he adds, 'I've written mainly about the bits of Spain in which the Abulafias generally did *not* live. Links between my family and Italy/Sicily did exist but I don't think they led me to Italian history. On the other hand, my interest in the meeting of cultures in the Mediterranean may well reflect my Sephardic background, as also my interest in merchant communities.'

VI

As much as an interest in European history among British historians may have been kindled by chance personal factors, it also owes something to longer-term influences. British historians of Italy came to the subject as inheritors of a long tradition of British fascination with the country, going back, as Christopher Duggan points out, as far as the eighteenth century. 'My attraction to Italian history', he writes, 'came initially, I think, from a childhood interest in the Renaissance, holidays to Italy, and time spent in the National Gallery (which is of course largely a product of the Grand Tour and its attendant cultural "special relationship" with Italy).' He points out that this special relationship took on a new and rather different lease of life during the unification of Italy in the nineteenth century, where it gained a second, political dimension. Thus British interest in Italian history is both cultural and political. Duggan suggests that 'the substantial group of specialists on modern Italy that have entered the academy since the 1950s . . . have probably all been in some degree products of the essentially romantic linkage of the UK to Italy that underlies both aspects of the "special relationship" (and which goes back beyond the Grand Tour era to the sixteenth century's heavy cultural borrowings)'. Travel to the country itself seems to have been particularly important, indeed, in sparking an interest in Italian history; far more so, for example, than in the case of Germany. Lucy Riall 'enjoyed visiting Continental Europe, wanted to know more about its history, and felt personally engaged with, and inspired by, questions about Italian identity' – this last factor a product, perhaps, of her upbringing in the Irish Republic. John Pollard's interest in the history of Italy was deepened by the experience of living and working there, teaching English in Padua after he abandoned a career in the civil service on deciding the life of an administrator was not for him.

A similar kind of attraction has been exerted by France. 'France', writes Peter Campbell, 'was impenetrable but desirable, a challenge to understand.' He went on regular caravanning holidays to France with his parents – 'pretty

French girl in next-door caravan, at 13, friendship, exchange, ice-skating with French girls at 15, broken French: France, *pays du désir!*' Robert Tombs pursued French history because, among other things, as a young man he 'fancied dossing around in Paris'. Olwen Hufton

> fell in love with France at the age of 15 during a school visit to Bayeux in Normandy, where we stayed in a convent. I subsequently – a year later – worked in another convent there with the English visitors and I had lots of time to read from their library. Boulanger's *Grand Siècle* I remember was one work that fired me and I couldn't wait to go to Versailles, where my pen friend was an extra in the film *Si Versailles m'était conté*. Normandy was/is full of everything from the Conqueror onwards.

William Doyle admits: 'It was simply the romance of a foreign culture, and the chance to live in it while I was working, which led me to work on France. Like, I suspect, a lot of other historians of France, part of the attraction was to get as far south as possible, and that is why I ended up in Bordeaux. How many Brits, I wonder', he asks rhetorically, 'have chosen to work in Lille, despite what I believe are very good archives?'

Of course, the reality could turn out to be something of a disappointment. For Christopher Clark, for instance, the attraction of following in the footsteps of the French medieval social historians like Emanuel Le Roy Ladurie was not merely intellectual: 'In my mind', he writes, '– and I can't have been alone in this – the idea of studying medieval France in the *Annales* tradition somehow became intertwined with the idea of reading novels in a warm sunlit corner of the Café

St. Germain.' But, he continues, 'happily I didn't stay on this track, because nothing in my fantasy could have prepared me for the squalor of professional academic life in today's Paris, or for the fact that a cup of coffee at the Café St. Germain costs half the weekly salary of a lecturer at Paris X-Nanterre'. Soon enough, indeed, he turned to modern German history instead, largely because he had a German girlfriend (whom he subsequently married) and the Free University of Berlin seemed to be the most convenient place for them to pursue their studies together. Once ensconced in Berlin, where the *Annales* school had barely been noticed, medieval history quickly came to seem dull, and modern history, present in the city on every street-corner, far more compelling.

Encountering the physical evidence of the past at an impressionable age can have a major effect. Leif Jerram was led to his topic by the built environment in which he studied: St Catherine's College, Oxford, a masterpiece of modern architecture by the Danish architect and designer Arne Jacobsen, whose European shape and structure, he writes, 'meant that I experienced, every day, "foreign" ideas about reason and space and social organisation'. Sir John Elliott originally 'decided to work on the history of Spain in large part as a result of the impression made on me by the country in the summer of 1950, during a Long Vacation trip at the end of my first year at Cambridge'. Peter Linehan was first attracted to his subject on a school visit to Spain in 1959. 'I was captivated not so much by the medieval cathedrals as by all the evidences of the Civil War', and on returning home read as much as he could about the subject; only later, when his attempt to do a PhD on the topic had run into the sands, did he go back seven centuries and begin his life's work, on the thirteenth century. More generally, however, David Abulafia probably speaks for many when he confesses that at least one reason for his decision to devote himself to the history of Spain and Italy was that 'I like warm, sunny places with good food, handsome buildings, fine vistas and cheerful inhabitants.'

Relatively few British historians who work on Germany, on the other hand, as Sir Ian Kershaw remarks, began with 'the sort of "love-affair" that many Brits have for France, Italy or Spain'. Instead, the interest of British historians has been sparked above all by intellectual challenges. My own personal history is a case in point. As an adolescent in the 1960s I became interested, predictably enough, in rebellion and revolution, and during my undergraduate years at Oxford I focused therefore on areas and periods of history that saw human beings break out of their humdrum and convention-bound lives. One such was the era of the Commonwealth and Protectorate at the end of the Civil Wars of seventeenth-century England, on which I took a document-based Special Subject (though somewhat to my disappointment, the documents focused far more on Cromwell's foreign policy, since his dealings with Jamaica and North America were held to be a key moment in the founding of the British Empire, whose celebration had still been a paramount purpose of the course when it had been set up some years before, than on rebellion and revolution; despite all the work of Christopher Hill and other radical historians on the Levellers, the Diggers, and similar revolutionary movements, the selection of set texts had evidently failed to move with the times).

Another was the Crusades, with which I had become virtually obsessed after reading Sir Steven Runciman's brilliant three-volume history, though I quickly realized I would never be able to become a researcher on them, because as a not very gifted linguist I would never be able to learn Arabic (and it seemed unfair to study the Crusades in depth without it). In modern history, Germany seemed to offer a good deal of upheaval and revolution of varying kinds that cried out for explanation, and German history was just opening up, with serious critical research on the long-term roots of Nazism beginning, and the whole question of long-term continuities in German history from the Nazis back through the Kaiser's Germany and beyond having been put on the agenda in no uncertain terms by the great German historian Fritz Fischer, whose visit to Oxford in 1989 was a dramatic and memorable occasion.

Crucial, however, were two new and, for people like me who had come of age amidst the optimism of the mid-1960s, disturbing and alarming developments on the world political stage. The first was the Vietnam War, which raised the question of why some countries engaged in military and imperialist wars that seemed on the face of it irrational and counter-productive; and the second was the rise of neo-fascism both in Germany and in the UK, with a new and vicious racism fuelled by the rabble-rousing speeches of the maverick Tory politician Enoch Powell. Why not, therefore, tackle the question of whether – as a German friend in Oxford never tired of speculating – Britain was going through a 'pre-fascist' phase, together with the question of why the Americans were in Vietnam, by looking at the long-term origins of Nazism and trying to pinpoint the moment when liberal values began to collapse in pre-Nazi German political culture? This reasoning led me to look for a liberal movement of social reform that was manageable enough in research terms to follow over quite a long period. I ended up with the feminist movement, whose history at that point, in the late 1960s, was almost completely unknown and unresearched, even in Germany, as I was soon to discover.

So while my own childhood had, as it were, put Germany on the agenda, it took the political conjuncture of '1968' to bring me to pick the country's history as a topic for research. A similar kind of political motivation played a role in the decision of Victoria Harris to take up German History. Active in American student politics at the start of George W. Bush's Presidency, she found that

> studying Germany helped me understand the historical context I found myself in, and since I had no personal ties to Germany it was a far less combative way to do it than exploring either of my own national contexts. After 9/11, meaningful dialogue about America's choices and history all but shut down, even within Brown's left-wing bubble. Studying Germany gave me a way out.

Among the possible alternatives, extra-European history seemed too obviously politically loaded, while 'growing up a foreigner in a very jingoistic society and having suffered through a good dose of propaganda made me averse to American history', she says.

The motives that have driven present-day British historians to study the Continent have thus been extremely varied. They range from present-day political preoccupations to indebtedness to the traditional factors that have often enticed Britons abroad – the lure of the Mediterranean in the case of many Italianists, a love of Russian literature in the case of many Russianists, an intellectual and political commitment among a number of Germanists, the romantic image of Paris or the South with many who have chosen France. To some extent, these motivations link up with those that drove the Victorians to engage with these foreign cultures: intellectual and philosophical in the case of Germany, for example, or the 'Mediterranean passion' in the case of Italianists. 'Our Europeanist historians of today', says Norman Davies,

> have much in common with the countless generations of
> British scholars and travellers who ventured abroad, 'went
> native', learned the local languages, and returned home
> to enrich the Mother Country with their exotic tales.
> As such, they were part of a wider phenomenon, dating
> back to the mercenary bands of the Hundred Years' War,
> the Merchant Adventurers, or imperialist explorers and
> travellers of the Victorian Age, attracted by the romance
> of non-British destinations.

Nevertheless, in modern times they could not have pursued their interest had it not been for the presence in British universities of institutional structures and individual, senior teachers and researchers encouraging them to do so. Moreover, as we saw in Chapter 1, they have taken to the countries they work on a strong reputation for objectivity and readability that has, with varying degrees, and depending on what they have been saying, ensured a reception for their work. None of this would have been possible, however, if they did not possess a mastery of European languages. This is not something for which the British are famous. How, then, have British Europeanists acquired it? Is this mastery no longer present amongst the younger generations of British historians? And if this is indeed the case, how do we account for this development, and what are its consequences for the continuation of the British tradition of writing and researching on the history of the European Continent? These are the topics to which we turn in the final chapter of this essay.

5

The language problem

I

Back in the 1950s and 1960s, you were required to have a knowledge of Latin and one other foreign language before you could even be considered for admission to read History at Oxford. The special entrance examination set by the History Faculty included passages for translation, and if you got in, you spent your first term – a mere eight weeks – studying not only Gibbon's *Decline and Fall of the Roman Empire* and Macaulay's *History of England* as contrasting examples of British historiography, but also (in my case) Alexis de Tocqueville's *L'Ancien Régime et la Révolution* and the Venerable Bede's *Historia ecclesiastica gentis anglorum*, whose medieval Latin came as something of a shock to anyone brought up on Cicero and Caesar. At the end of the term, in order to be allowed to proceed to take the rest of the three-year degree in Modern History, you had to pass the Preliminary Examination, which included passages from these, or other, similar works chosen from a brief list of approved texts, set for translation into English and commentary on their historical meaning and significance.

Document-based Special Subjects, which provided a final-year stepping-stone to research, required intensive study of extracts, or 'gobbets', from original texts in French, Latin, German, Italian or whatever language they had been written in, depending on what the subject was; in order to take the Special Subject on the Third Reich, for instance, introduced in the 1970s, Oxford undergraduates had to have a good working knowledge of German. Even in non-document-based subjects, knowledge of a foreign language was often required. My Tutor for the history of the Crusades, Maurice Keen, for example, frequently sent me to obscure Latin chronicles of the lesser-known Crusades printed in a vast nineteenth-century compilation, Migne's *Patrologia latina*, whose serried ranks of volumes seemed to fill a whole wall in the library. He did not appear to think I would experience any difficulty reading through them.

Of course, says Robert Anderson, 'the past should not be idealized too much'. When he was at school, 'French was taught, in classic British fashion, as a dead language. There was no spoken element at all, and I was able to take O levels without being able to conduct a simple conversation.' The emphasis was on grammar and literature, and colloquial language was avoided. Nevertheless, he says, in the 1950s and 1960s it was generally believed 'that an educated person should have a wide range of interests for which the school syllabus was only a foundation, and that this should include catching up with foreign languages and cultures'. Undergraduates at many British universities in the 1950s and 1960s were assumed to have a good reading knowledge of at least one foreign language because languages were a core part of the school curriculum of the day, in state schools as well as in the independent sector. Almost all British specialists on Continental European history learned languages at school; some indeed, as we have seen, came to their chosen country's history mainly through love of its language. In many cases, they already knew more than one language and, for almost all of them, an interest in learning languages proved crucial. Guy Rowlands had Italian and German as well as French. As a pupil at St Paul's School in London, David Abulafia learned Latin, Greek, French and German ('In those days it was clearly understood at St. Paul's that anyone planning to read History at a leading university should have a command of several languages'). 'I picked up a good reading knowledge of Catalan, Castilian and Portuguese', he adds, 'as my research moved towards Spain and Portugal, though I have never followed courses in these languages.'

Norman Davies notes that 'language learning took a prominent place in my education from start to finish'. Growing up in Bolton, he cultivated 'a romantic enthusiasm for everything Welsh' as a boy, drawing on his father's Welsh roots, and while his early efforts to learn the notoriously difficult Welsh language came to nothing, this gave him 'a feel for wrestling with non-English idioms'. He was taught French at school, was 'introduced both to Italian, by my History master, with whom we toured Italy, and to a lesser extent to Russian, by an assistant geography master who harboured a mysterious passion for the Soviet Union. As a student and a young graduate', he recalls, 'I could have been best described as a collector of languages. I moved from French and Italian into Spanish, and spent vacations at summer schools at Prague and Bucharest, dabbling with Czech and Romanian', to which he later added Polish. 'My one failure', he confesses, 'was with German, where I encountered an unexpected emotional block. My distaste for the language, and my inability to tackle it successfully, probably derived from family stories about a much-loved uncle who had been maltreated in a wartime German camp and from associations with an ex-girlfriend who had been studying German when she unceremoniously threw me out.'

Norman Davies was not alone in his ability to collect languages. In a younger generation, for example, Robert Frost studied French and Latin at school and took Russian to avoid having to do science, 'hung out quite a lot with language students' at university 'and started teaching myself German in the long summer vacations when I was a porter on the back door in my father's shop (long hours of tedium)'. He learned Polish in order to do his PhD, 'learnt Italian through reading the papal nuncio's reports with a dictionary (not too hard if you have French and Latin) . . . learnt Swedish, and can get by in Ukrainian, Belarussian and Czech, as well as Danish. I am now learning Lithuanian. It is', he adds, somewhat surprisingly after this lengthy catalogue, 'hard.' A lucky few, like these, possess an innate ability to pick up languages of almost any kind seemingly with a minimum of effort. For most of us, it's a good deal more difficult. But learning a language at school provides a kind of framework for acquiring other European languages later on in life, since the basic structures and rules are more or less the same in most cases.

'ANY language is a start', declares Catherine Merridale, noting that it was her fluency in French that set her on the road to her eventual mastery of Russian. Similarly, Robert Service studied Classics at school and knew Latin and Ancient Greek before he embarked on a degree in Medieval and Modern Languages at Cambridge, learning Russian from scratch but not finding it difficult because of his knowledge of Classical languages. The same principle has held true from my own experience in the 1960s and early 1970s to that of Victoria Harris in the early 2000s, who notes that she had learned French and Latin at school, 'so I didn't find German very difficult to learn' later on. Quite a few British historians of Continental Europe, indeed, learned the language they needed not at school, but specifically in order to research for their doctorate. I had no knowledge at all of German when I decided, on graduating from Oxford, to do a doctorate in German History. But I had French and Latin, and though I'm no linguistic genius, German is a logical and relatively straightforward language, and after making a rather shaky start with *Teach Yourself German*, I was able to master it in four months of intensive residential language courses put on by the Goethe Institute in Germany. At that time, the government funding bodies (in my case the then Social Science Research Council) were willing to support two months of these (rather expensive) courses, and I was lucky enough to win a financial grant for a further two months thanks to an enterprising don who approached the Federal German Chancellor Willy Brandt when he was awarded an Honorary Degree at Oxford and asked him what he could do for the University and its students in return.

II

Historians of European countries have often been obliged to learn the language or languages they need when they first embark on their research because it has sometimes been frustratingly difficult to study a country's history along with its language at the same time at school or university in Britain. When Patrick Major opted to learn German at school, for instance, he was forced to drop History in order to do so. Kevin Passmore had O-level French but 'was not allowed to take A level French' because he was studying History instead, 'went to Warwick because it was one of the few good universities that did not require an A Level language', and did not learn French properly until after he graduated, using Linguaphone tapes. Despite the daunting examples of historians like Robert Evans, Norman Davies or Robert Frost, you do not have to be particularly linguistically gifted to study the history of a country where English is not the native language. Sometimes the challenge of doing something difficult is a spur in itself. David Moon, for instance, learned Russian while a postgraduate student in Birmingham. He had O-level German when he left school, and one of the reasons why he chose to study Russian history was because 'I felt this would be a challenge as foreign languages had been my weakest academic subject at secondary school.'

'I'm no born linguist', admits Mary Laven, 'and, to be honest, part of the appeal of Italian was that you can go a long way by adding a vowel to words used in English. For my doctoral project, once I'd mastered "cattolicismo", "la controriforma", and "convento femminile", I was nearly home and dry. These days', she adds, 'I try to convince would-be graduate students that reading documents in Italian will not be the greatest challenge that they face.' Nevertheless, it helped that she had picked up a good deal of the language during family holidays and a gap year in Venice. No doubt her experience was the same in many ways as that of her brother David Laven, who 'had no formal training in Italian and no qualification beyond a self-taught O-level. What I knew I had acquired from grammars, voracious but ill-directed and unsystematic reading, and, later, chatting in bars and archives.' Nevertheless, in the end, at least some work is required. 'I periodically seethe', he goes on, 'when British historians announce that I am "lucky" to have foreign languages. There is no luck about it, simply a consequence of varying degrees of application.'

The majority of British historians of Continental Europe whom I questioned learned the necessary language or languages either at school, at university (as part of a Language or European Studies degree or a joint degree in History and Language) or in a language school abroad; only a few were, for one reason or another, brought up bilingually. Almost all the British historians of Continental Europe who responded to my questionnaire, however, note that they only really achieved mastery of their languages by living in the countries where they were spoken. Robert Tombs picked up 'a bit' of French at school, but learned the language 'mainly by going to France and getting jobs, making friends, and learning on the spot'. Sir John Elliott could read Spanish, thanks to a summer course for foreigners in Santiago de Compostela, mastered the spoken language during a year's research in Spain, and 'learned Catalan by taking lodging with a Catalan family in Barcelona and asking them to speak to me only in Catalan'. Chris Ealham 'picked up Spanish and Catalan after I started my doctoral work'. This, he notes, 'was rendered easier by having studied French at school'. A-level Latin enabled Peter

Linehan to teach himself Spanish, though he adds, 'alarm bells still ring if I sense an imperfect subjunctive in the vicinity'.

Peter Campbell picked up some French as a boy on family holidays in France, and took A-level French, which enabled him to study French-language documents in his university Special Subject, but he learned to speak the language properly only during his doctoral research in Paris, largely through French friends (usually the quickest way to learn a language). Leif Jerram had French but no German, so 'I bought *German in Three Months* (a lie) and went and got a job as an English teacher in Bremen (a universally saleable skill not open to speakers of other languages). My first attempt to buy a tram ticket', he confesses, 'led the tram driver to ask if I spoke English.' Fluency in a foreign tongue generally only comes through being forced to speak as well as read; it's vital for dealing with monoglot archivists and librarians, landladies, shop assistants and the like, and generally necessary for survival during prolonged research trips.

More than that, a really thorough command of the languages is absolutely indispensable when it comes to deciphering handwritten sources, since you often have to guess the meaning of illegible words from the surrounding sentences. In some languages the difficulties are even more severe; Cyrillic script is still used in Russia and some other parts of Eastern Europe, for instance, while German handwriting before the Second World War is in a completely different hand known as *Sütterlin*, which has to be taught to researchers before they can tackle the archives, and even printed German is in Gothic typeface, which takes a good deal of getting used to. These additional problems and challenges can easily lead to disaster.

When I was researching in the German Federal Archives in Koblenz in the early 1970s, for example, a particularly malevolent reading-room supervisor used to persecute mercilessly the odd American PhD student whose German was too shaky for him to be able to answer back, and I knew at least one of them who was almost driven to despair by the treatment he received. More seriously, one young American never did find the time or inspiration to learn how to read the *Sütterlin*, and completed his dissertation, on the history of one of the major political parties in Imperial Germany, on the basis of printed and typewritten sources only, thus leaving out vital manuscript material and rendering it more or less useless to scholarship.

For historians of early modern and, still more, of course, medieval Europe, the problems posed by handwritten sources are even more acute, and a complete knowledge of the language in which they are written becomes even more essential. And to hold one's own in a foreign language in a seminar, conference or lecture-hall can be an even greater challenge: academic French, for example, is a different, more complex, more abstract language than its everyday counterpart, and has to be mastered if one is to be taken seriously. Peter Campbell only really learned it in 1990 through sharing a flat in Paris with a French academic. Now, teaching part of every year at a French university, he notes: 'I improvise my French classes at Versailles from notes, just as I do in England. I have no idea how the thought-processes work, and again that mystery is part of the anthropological fascination with the "other", the hard-to-understand, the indecipherable.'

Some projects require a knowledge of not one foreign language but several. This applies not only to comparative, transnational or intercultural history, but also to the history of key states and political systems in the European past. For many centuries, for example, the Habsburg Monarchy was one of Europe's great powers. Yet writing its history presents formidable linguistic obstacles to the researcher. In the Preface to his magisterial work *The Habsburg Empire, 1789–1918*, published in 1968, C. A. Macartney recalled that, during his time in Vienna after the First World War, he had tried to read up about 'the past of the great Monarchy among whose still-smoking ruins I had arrived', but found that there was no satisfactory, comprehensive general narrative history of the subject:

> I conceived the ambition of writing the story myself. In 1925 (I think) I talked to the distinguished Austrian historian, A. F. Pribram, and told him of my ambition. I still remember his answer. 'Yes, we all start with that ambition. I did myself, but gave it up because I did not know fourteen languages.' I did not myself know anything like fourteen languages, and felt rebuked for my presumption . . . I put my ambition aside and waited for someone better qualified than myself to produce the book which I wanted to see. But I have waited for forty years. So much material has appeared during those years that an attempt to write such a book as I had in mind would no longer be absurd . . . I still do not know fourteen languages . . . But man cannot wait for ever, either on his own perfection, or on others, so I have decided to face the world with my effort, imperfect as I know it to be.

The crucial languages for such an undertaking are German and Hungarian, both of which Macartney knew inside-out;

but Czech, Polish, Romanian and Italian also certainly help as well. Historians who decide to study the Habsburg Monarchy are usually, it seems scarcely necessary to say, linguistically talented, and a love of languages is in fact sometimes the spur, as with Robert Evans, whose book *The Making of the Habsburg Monarchy* is one of the classics in the field.

Alan Sked, author of *The Survival of the Habsburg Empire: Radetzky, the Imperial Army and the Class War, 1848* (1979) and a much-reprinted study, *The Decline and Fall of the Habsburg Empire, 1815–1918* (2nd edition, 2001), turned to European History initially because he wanted to learn German, having already mastered Latin, Greek and French at school. On graduating from Oxford, he decided to do a doctorate there in Habsburg history. This, he thought, would force him to learn German. How, then, did he learn it?

> I taught myself. I needed German, Italian and Hungarian, but also discovered that I needed to learn nineteenth-century *Handschrift* [handwriting], which, of course, no-one in Oxford had warned me about. Indeed, when I eventually secured a supervisor ('Would you *mind* if we gave you to A. J. P. Taylor?', asked a weary Freddy Madden of the Oxford Faculty Board), I discovered that my lack of knowledge of German might scupper the whole enterprise. 'No German? Can't be done!' exclaimed Taylor at our first meeting, before handing me a copy of Redlich's 800-page Gothic tome on *Das Oesterreichische Staats- und Rechtsproblem* and telling me to come back when I had read it. Three weeks later, I astonished him when I returned to say that if the middle was as boring as the introduction and conclusion, I did not intend to read

any more of it. I later discovered in his autobiography that in 1934 he himself had gone off to Vienna to do what was in fact his doctoral thesis there – without knowing any German!

It is scarcely surprising, he adds, that 'since the Habsburgs seem a historical dead-end and require a good knowledge of languages and geography to study properly, few people undertake research in the area'.

Even when a historian focuses, more modestly, on the history of a single European country, there may still be linguistic traps lurking for the unwary. Anyone wanting to study Italian history, particularly before the unification of the nineteenth century, must, for example, depending on what part of Italy comes into question, know one or more languages apart from Italian. 'French is essential for nineteenth-century Italian history', notes Lucy Riall, 'as much private and official correspondence is in French.' German is equally essential for students of Tuscany and Venetia in the eighteenth century, ruled from Vienna as part of the Habsburg Monarchy. French is needed for the study of eighteenth-century Germany and Russia, unless you are doing really grass-roots social history. In this case, students of Prussian society have to master the obscure low-German dialect in which many key local documents are written. In multilingual Hungary, Latin remained the official language even into the nineteenth century. And if you want to study early medieval history, says Rosamond McKitterick, and master the historiography as well as the sources, 'one has to have Latin, German, French, and if possible Italian, plus the language of whatever country on whose history one chooses to specialise'. Thus 'those without the incentive or effort to learn a foreign language then limit their horizons and opportunities unnecessarily'. All of these factors are further challenges, or, for some, deterrents. These linguistic challenges are particularly important at a time when language-learning in Britain has entered a period of severe and perhaps terminal crisis.

III

The rapid and continuing decline of language-learning in British schools is in many ways the most important single factor threatening the continuation of the long tradition of British historians' engagement with the European Continent. 'Without foreign languages', declares Robert Service, 'the threat to our existing standing in Continental historiography is going to be lethal.' History at A-level, the main qualifying examination for university entrance, in schools in England and Wales, has more or less held its own over the past decade or so, with entries declining only slightly from 47,900 in 1996–7 to 45,400 in 2006–7. But entries for Modern Languages at A-level have declined precipitously, from 52,000 in 1996–7 to 31,100 in 2006–7. The number of students taking French at A-level has fallen from 28,800 to 13,700, the number taking German from 12,100 to 6,000, in both cases a fall of more than half. Only Spanish has held its own, with 5,900 candidates in 1996–7 and 6,000 in 2006–7; and the overall fall has been cushioned very slightly by the take-up for non-European languages such as Mandarin Chinese, Hindi or Urdu. Overall, however, the traditional European languages are fast disappearing from our schools, a process hastened by the British government's decision that pupils need no longer learn any foreign language at all throughout their studies up to GCSE (the examination taken two years before A-level). Universities have responded by relaxing and then abolishing the requirement that candidates for entry should have mastered any language apart from English, and the decline in qualified entrants has led to one Language Department after another at universities being merged or closed down altogether. This process has inevitably had a knock-on effect for postgraduate studies too.

Not surprisingly, therefore, Sir Ian Kershaw has

> the distinct impression that the numbers of native British students working on Continental themes has declined fairly sharply since the heyday of the 1960s and 1970s. The current generation of British historians is, I think, struggling to reproduce itself and, apart from the 'Golden Triangle' [of Oxford, Cambridge and London] (and even here, much of the graduate work seems to be that of native Germans or offspring of German émigrés etc.), the numbers working on Continental history appear to be very small.

Catherine Merridale, indeed, despairs of finding British students to engage in research on the history of Continental countries and urges us all 'to encourage students from the EU to do research with us (and students from Russia), since they are often the only ones who CAN do original research'. This is indeed happening. Eight out of the fifteen PhD students I have supervised to completion at Cambridge have been Germans (with three Canadians and one Swiss national, so only a minority of them have been British). At Reading, Christopher Duggan reports that 'almost all my PhD students in the last fifteen years have been from Italy'. 'If things go on at the present rate', observes Robert Service, lamenting the decline of language-learning in the British education system, 'we shall have a permanent need of . . . youngish Germans to staff our Continental history programmes for want of adequate training of the indigenous, woad-painted Britons.'

Is the national paradigm breaking down, then? 'We Europeanists', Catherine Merridale says, 'need to be more generous in reading across Europe – not bedding down in our language/region areas but trying to engage in a discourse that includes comparison and debate with others.' The fact that knowledge of a range of languages is needed to do this gives a strong advantage to students from the European Continent, who routinely read and speak two or three other languages apart from English and their own. As Norman Davies observes, the continuing popular demand for good, broadly conceived books on European history

> is likely to increase. At the same time, the shortages of supply could well be remedied by the huge influx of foreigners to British academia. These newcomers do not suffer from the linguistic deprivation of many young Britons and Americans, and they may conceivably be attracted by neglected British traditions. When my Polish colleagues complain that their country's history is frequently ignored or mangled abroad, I tell them that they must produce another Joseph Conrad, with a historical bent. And the advice could apply to many countries. What is certain is that the next generation of historians

in Britain is going to be considerably more international, cosmopolitan and multiracial than the last one. And there is a good chance that the new mix of youngsters will throw up the stars to feed the historical hunger.

Christopher Duggan, similarly, notes that 'the absence of jobs for young historians in Italy has meant a steady influx from Italy of PhD students of the highest quality; and the teaching of Italian history in UK universities in the future may depend largely on them'.

Lucy Riall, too, observes that 'much of the generation that is younger than me comes from the European countries which are being studied'. Tim Kirk notes that 'appointments to posts in European History (including Ancient History and Archaeology) at Newcastle in the last five years have been nationals of European countries (Spain, Italy, Germany, France). Lack of language skills among potential postgrads is the main problem.' In Edinburgh, Jill Stephenson has noted a tendency over the past few years

> to appoint native German-speakers to positions in
> German History (but also in other specialisms – we have
> had Germans in US History and the History of Islam,
> and we have now appointed Italians in both African and
> Renaissance History) . . . The last time we interviewed for
> a permanent post in (early modern) European History,
> four of the five short-listed were non-British (continental
> Europeans) – Italian (who was appointed), Greek,
> Dutch and German, and one Brit. For the previous
> (later modern) European post, we appointed two people,
> a Finn and a first-generation Brit whose parents are
> Spanish.

Patrick Major reckons that more than three-quarters of new appointments in the History Department at Warwick University in the last ten years have been non-British, and his younger colleagues in History at Reading, where he has just taken up a Chair, include Italians and Dutch. He concludes that 'British academia's very openness to outside influences . . ., which I generally applaud, is in danger of leading to a division of labour in which British historians give up on catering for foreign history. Instead we will simply import the historians.'

Paradoxically, therefore, there is a continued demand in British universities for European History, but the British students who engage with it are not entering the profession in sufficient numbers, and the teaching is being supplied increasingly by Continental Europeans. 'Will modern Europeanists in UK [History] Departments be in large part Germans (some of whom did their PhDs in the UK) within 10–20 years?' asks Tim Cole. The EU certainly makes a difference here: students from member states can get a grant from the Arts and Humanities Research Council (AHRC) to do postgraduate research at a British university, and the single labour market has made it easier than before for young historians from the rest of the EU to apply for teaching jobs. Thus, for example, surveying the applications from historians for the coveted Junior Research Fellowships offered jointly by Churchill, Fitzwilliam and Murray Edwards Colleges and Trinity Hall in Cambridge for October 2009, John Pollard notes that 38 out of 112 were in European History; 23 of these latter came from non-British applicants.

Some indication of the change more generally can be gained from looking at the list of officers and committee members of the German History Society, founded in 1979 to bring British specialists in the field together in conferences and, subsequently, to run a journal, *German History*, to subsidize postgraduate research, and to award grants and prizes. In 1983–4, the fifteen officers and committee members consisted of William Carr, Anthony Glees, Dick Geary, David Blackbourn, Richard Evans, John Flood, Mary Fulbrook, John Hiden, Gerhard Hirschfeld, Joe Lee, Anthony Nicholls, Jeremy Noakes, Bob Scribner, Jill Stephenson and Simon Steyne. The only German in the list, Gerhard Hirschfeld, was there in his capacity as a Fellow of the German Historical Institute in London, in order to liaise between the Society and the Institute. In 2008–9, the twelve officers and committee members were Stefan Berger, Annika Mombauer, Corey Ross, Paul Betts, Maiken Umbach, Jeannette Madarasz, Kerstin Brückweh, Beat Kümin, Josie McLellan, Christina von Hodenberg, Matthew Stibbe and Chris Szejnmann. Germans were in the majority and there were only two Britons.

Alex Bamji reports that 'for the two lectureships in Early Modern European History I've been shortlisted for, half or more candidates have been from outside the UK'. This trend is especially strong amongst young historians from Italy and Germany; particularly in the latter country, it takes far longer than in the UK to gain the qualifications needed to teach in a university, and jobs are in extremely short supply. The same is not true of their French counterparts. As Peter Jones, speaking from many years' experience of working in France, notes, 'I am struck, even today, by how reluctant the French are to travel and uproot themselves even within their own country. It can't be a coincidence', he observes, 'that I have lots of young German nationals as colleagues here in Birmingham, but scarcely a single French man or woman.' Nevertheless, despite the reluctance of the French, the overall trend is unmistakable. 'Unless language teaching in the UK is enhanced', warns Jonathan Osmond, who teaches German and European History at Cardiff, 'British expertise will be restricted to very few persons.'

The migration of young Continental Europeans to British universities as students and teachers is undoubtedly an implicit compliment to the well-organized, open and (on the whole) rationally structured nature of British Higher Education. Could it also be seen as a problem? Some think it is, particularly when it comes to sustaining the British tradition of writing for a broad readership in a literary style. Yet a surprisingly large number of German and other students decide to take not only their postgraduate but also their undergraduate studies at British universities. Of the PhD students I have supervised, for instance, Nik Wachsmann and Jan Rüger studied at the LSE, Bernhard Fulda at Oxford, Christian Goeschel at York, Dan Vyleta at Cambridge and Tom Neuhaus at Essex before coming on to do graduate work with me, and thus all of them have had no exposure to Higher Education except in the UK. Moreover, even with those who have come directly from German universities, four or five years of taking a Master's degree and a PhD in the intensive and distinctive historical culture that surrounds them at Cambridge or elsewhere undeniably has an effect on the way they approach their work. Adjustment may be more difficult in the case of established scholars who come directly from Continental countries to fill posts in British universities, but even here, student expectations will surely have an effect in getting them to adapt. The key difference may be in the area of writing and publication, where older imported historians often prefer to continue writing and publishing in their own native language. By contrast, those who have trained in the UK as either undergraduates or postgraduates often have an enviably stylish and fluent way with the English language by the time they finish: the books, developed from their PhD theses, by Jan Rüger and Nik Wachsmann, for instance, will stand comparison for breadth, scope and read-ability with any work published by their British peers, while Dan Vyleta has gone on from his academic work to produce a major novel, *Pavel and I*, in English, that has won wide-spread critical acclaim.

There are many reasons for the dwindling supply of young Britons to research and teach European history. Guy Rowlands for one has 'noticed since leaving Oxbridge that in universities employing much more continuous assess-ment of coursework there is greater reluctance by students to have a go at foreign language material, for fear of getting lower marks'. This carries through to the postgraduate level. 'Bright students coming through the History BA and MA programme', observes Miriam Dobson, at Sheffield, 'often specialize in Russian history at undergraduate level but then realize that the task of acquiring Russian is going to put them at a disadvantage compared to students focusing on British history.' Yet, on the other hand, neither William Doyle nor Guy Rowlands has noticed any fall in the numbers of post-graduates who are members of the Society for the Study of French History. Similarly, Mary Laven has the impression 'that the British tradition of European history is holding up relatively well despite the erosion of language learning in schools. There is', she thinks 'a steady stream of excellent graduate students attracted to the field. Indeed', she goes on, 'one could argue that our graduate students are pre-selected to be (a) especially driven and (b) intellectually flexible, since they have avoided the "easy" option of working on exclusively Anglophone sources, and they have shown a commitment to spending time abroad – experiencing as well as studying another culture.'

Norman Davies is also relatively optimistic. 'It is often said these days', he notes, 'that the established British tradition of writing European History is an endangered species.' However, he goes on:

> I'm not so sure. History learning in general is under threat, due to new educational priorities. And history-writing as a narrative art and as a branch of *belles-lettres* falls increasingly out of fashion. Philistine professionals apply themselves ever more obsessively to mere research or to academic disputation. It is particularly deplorable that the study of modern languages in British schools is declining rapidly, inevitably narrowing both the opportunities and the mental horizons of young scholars. Yet the production of well-written, mega-surveys of important European topics does not appear to be drying up. And they find their readership.

'What can be done about the problem?' he asks: 'The only answer which I have is to try and set a good example.'

IV

In the 1960s, a number of the universities newly founded in the wake of the expansion of Higher Education advocated by the Robbins report attempted to break the traditional disciplinary mould and establish themselves on the basis of large, multidisciplinary Schools of Study. One such was the University of East Anglia, where I taught from 1976 to 1989. There was no History Department as such; instead, the economic historians were put together with the economists and sociologists in a School of Social Sciences, the English and American historians were located with literature specialists in a School of English and American Studies, and European historians such as myself shared the School of European Studies with teachers of French, German, Russian and Scandinavian languages and literatures. This had the advantage for Europeanists that one could expect undergraduates to be able to read a foreign language, since in effect they were all doing joint degrees, albeit with varying emphases (either in Literature or History). So I could get them to read original German-language sources for their undergraduate dissertations, and I could expect them to have a good knowledge of Germany and other Continental countries even before they embarked on the study of their histories.

But within a very short space of time things began to change. In the harsher economic climate of the 1980s, students began to see European languages not as a means of studying the literature or history of another culture, but as a route to a job. Soon we were having to counter a precipitous fall in applications for places by shifting the emphasis of our degrees to the study of contemporary Europe and putting on new courses combining languages with business studies (interesting, but not really what I wanted to do, so I left for a post in a History Department in London). Even this failed to stop the rot, however, and soon it was clear that students were ceasing to want to learn languages at all. So, not long after I left, the School was wound up, the historians left to join a new School of History, the literati migrated to English and American Studies, and a rump stayed on to provide language teaching services to other parts of the university. The interdisciplinary dream was over.

A similar story could be told of the University of Sussex, at Brighton, where the grand foundational ambition of creating a new mix of disciplines eventually collapsed in ruins as well. Patrick Major, who left the University of Warwick after many years to take up a Chair at Reading University, admits that 'one reason for leaving Warwick was a sense that its early commitment under founding chairs such as John Hale to a European dimension was fast disappearing'. Joint degrees in History and Modern Languages exist in many universities, but they cater only for a very small minority, and a good number of those who take, say, French and History, are themselves French native-speakers. These developments have a discernible effect on History. As a result of the decline of language-learning in the UK, the quality of the learning experience in British universities has declined when it comes to European History. Whereas a generation ago an undergraduate taking a Special Subject on Dante, as Norman Davies notes, was required to read the *Divine Comedy* in medieval Italian, and students tackling a document-based course on

Nazi Germany had no choice but to read the source-material in the original German, nowadays if you put on a course that requires this degree of competence in a foreign language you are likely to get few if any takers, and, as a result, you will come under heavy pressure from departmental and university administrators to close the course down.

David Moon points out that European History 'remains a popular subject among undergraduates at the UK universities I have taught at; however, very few students have a sufficient reading knowledge of a European language, or indeed the confidence in using the knowledge they do have, to engage in more advanced study at undergraduate or postgraduate level'. Working from translated documents is the solution adopted by most university teachers in the field, and unless you are prepared to spend many weeks translating them yourself, this drastically restricts the range of subjects you can teach through the study of historical documents. As so often, it is Nazi Germany that comes out on top, with many widely available printed collections of translated documents, headed by Jeremy Noakes's superb four-volume *Nazism 1919–1945: A Documentary History*, published by Exeter University Press. It's possible to do the same with topics like the French or Russian Revolutions or the Origins of the First World War, but stray very far from such well-worn tracks into new or uncharted territory, and you will have to do the work of translation yourself. Some translations are very good and very serviceable for teaching, of course, but they can never really convey all the subtleties, still less the real historical flavour, of texts in the original German, French, Italian, Russian or Spanish, and so the learning experience is subtly narrowed and diminished. Moreover, document-based Special Subjects were originally intended as a kind of bridge to postgraduate research, teaching the basics of source-criticism and the interpretation of historical documents. This link has now largely broken down, because reading documents in translation, however well it is done, is in the end no preparation at all for reading them in the language in which they were originally written, a task that every postgraduate history researcher has to grapple with from the very outset.

There have been further institutional changes at the postgraduate level that have had a discernible effect, in the eyes of many British Europeanists, in deterring students from undertaking doctorates where the source material is in a foreign language and the documents are located in foreign archives. Over the last decade or so, the nature of government funding for PhD research has changed dramatically, with the autonomous British Academy, which for many years provided grants from resources provided by the then Department of Education, giving way to the AHRC, which joined the other, science-oriented Research Councils, under the aegis of the then Department for Trade and Industry, in 2005. The closer integration with government has brought rapidly increasing pressure to deliver value for money.

Long gone are the days when PhD supervisors barely saw their students from one end of the year to the other, and graduates took six or eight years to complete a doctorate, if indeed they ever managed to complete it at all. Back in the early 1990s I remember one (admittedly part-time) PhD candidate at London University who had taken thirty-six years

213

to complete his PhD, spanning his entire career as a school-teacher from start to finish. Of course, only the first three years of a full-time PhD were ever funded by a grant, so if you had not completed by the time it ran out, you were faced with the prospect of trying to carry on with it while holding down a job, and inevitably it then took a back seat even if the job was in academia, causing lengthy delays. 'I started my PhD in 1987', remembers Alison Rowlands, 'and finished it in 1994 (getting teaching experience along the way).' Since her thesis was based heavily on difficult manuscript sources written in sixteenth-century German, this was scarcely surprising. 'I would be seen as a disaster now in terms of the length of time taken', she admits, 'but this period of research and living in Germany was necessary to me in order to develop as a scholar.' Her experience is far from untypical.

The AHRC is now demanding that 85 per cent of doctoral projects it funds in any given University Department must be brought to a successful conclusion within four years, whatever happens, or it will blacklist the offending Department by refusing to award it any further doctoral grants until it can demonstrate that it has mended its ways. PhD students are monitored at every point of their project, and supervision has become a far more rigorous and demanding activity than it used to be. Students are no longer thrown in at the deep end without any training when they begin. They have to take a Master's degree first, involving a varying amount of coursework and a short dissertation to be completed in a few months, to show they can research under pressure of time; they are put through research training courses of various kinds; and they are regularly checked and monitored throughout their doctoral studies. Supervision has become far more demanding and professional than it ever was in the past.

All of this is not only absolutely understandable and inevitable but also absolutely right. The waste of taxpayers' money on idle, badly supervised PhD students in the past was indefensible. And the threat of sanctions has been effective. Over the past three years, for example, over 85 per cent of AHRC-funded History PhDs in Cambridge have been completed within the required four-year period. Yet these changes have been bought at the price of a fundamental transformation of the PhD itself. In the past, a doctoral dissertation was regarded in effect as a first book; students were not discouraged from taking on a large or ambitious topic. Now, however, it is regarded increasingly as a test of the student's ability to do research, not as a major piece of research in itself. The topic must not be so broad or ambitious that it will require more than three or at most four years to complete. And this means that funding priority is given to projects that are carefully delimited and sharply focused – or, to put it in a less positive way, narrowly conceived and highly specialized. This works to the disadvantage of students wanting to research on European history. Not all of them, as we have seen, come to their topic with a command of the relevant language that is good enough to take them straight into the archives; most perfect it while doing their research, and this is becoming even more the case as the teaching and learning of languages in British schools and universities declines.

'Pressure to complete in a short time', warns Elizabeth Harvey, 'allows no leeway for learning a language and spending longish stints abroad.' Sir Ian Kershaw agrees: 'The pressure to complete a PhD in three years', he notes, 'makes it extremely difficult for a postgraduate to undertake systematic research in foreign archives after, most usually, having had to learn or master a foreign language, and produce a high-quality dissertation.' The main result of these pressures has been, as David Abulafia observes, that 'bodies such as the AHRC appear to be giving priority to the funding of historical projects with a British relevance'. 'The majority of our PhD students', writes Jill Stephenson from Edinburgh University,

> opt for British, Scottish, American or British colonial History (where the sources are often in English – although the very occasional student learns an Indian language). Those who study a European subject are more likely to have taken an undergraduate degree involving a language – we've recently had French and History and Italian graduates completing history PhDs. Those who have gone on to PhD from my taught Master's on The Second World War in Europe have all opted for British/Scottish History subjects connected with the war for their PhD.

'If we want to continue producing PhD dissertations on European topics', then, as Patrick Major warns, 'funding bodies may have to give two years of language acquisition time where learners spend the second year "in-country"', or, as Robert Tombs and others advocate, provide four years' support instead of three.

Even this suggestion assumes that only one foreign country will be the object of study. In the early twenty-first century, the history of the nation-state is increasingly giving way to global, transnational, intercultural and comparative history at the cutting edge of research, and this means mastery of not one foreign language, but several. In my own experience of supervising PhDs, it has invariably been the case that a project based on one country (Germany) has taken between three and four years, a project based on two has taken between four and five, and a project based on three between five and six. Nor have dissertations that took a long time been over-ambitious or poorly focused. One student whose work I supervised, Hugo Service, wrote on 'ethnic cleansing' in postwar Poland, a topic that inevitably requires a knowledge of two languages, since by definition it involves two ethnicities; he began with a decent command of German but had to learn Polish (in Germany, through the medium of German) as he was going along; he took just over five years to complete.

This kind of project has an obvious contemporary relevance. Yet it is virtually impossible to pursue such research any longer in the light of the increasingly draconian sanctions applied to Departments that allow PhD students to carry on researching for more than four years. As a result, as Geoffrey Hosking remarks, nowadays, 'doctoral theses . . . tend to be safe and cautious', a view shared by Chris Ealham, who says that 'the new PhD regulations . . . encourage conservatism, both among doctoral students (prospective and actual), and probably among supervisors'. Thus students, often acting on their supervisor's advice, increasingly avoid even considering embarking on ambitious projects, let alone undertaking them. Edward Acton was 'struck when serving on the AHRC postgraduate scholarship panel by the relative paucity and weakness of applications coming through

217

on Continental European history. Ring-fenced funding', or in other words the reservation of a specific number of grants for PhDs in European History, he suggests, 'is one important defensive measure. A sustained outgrowing of post-modernist trivialization of history', he adds, somewhat polemically, 'is another. So long as the British [historians] were content to fritter the tiny number of Research Council doctorates in history on [narrow and sometimes seemingly trivial] subjects, . . . the case for Continental vantage points was gravely weakened, along with that for comparative and serious history of all kinds.'

David Laven also considers that the difficulties of carrying out doctoral research in a foreign country should be recognized by a lengthier period of funding. 'It is outrageous and absurd that someone doing a PhD on potato-growing in Little Snoring gets the same funding for the same period as someone looking at several decades of government policy in pre-*Ausgleich* Hungary.' Those who actually do opt for European topics sometimes find ways round these problems that seriously reduce the value of their work. 'Too often', he adds,

> when postgraduates work on Continental subjects, they opt for fields in which there is already a large secondary literature rather than exploring new avenues. This turns the PhD into a largely historiographical exercise, producing dull history and failing to develop the necessary archival skills to do exciting work later in a career. Or PhDs become dominated by the application of modish methodologies rather than worthwhile and lasting exploration of original sources.

These are perhaps problems that can be dealt with by taking care to devise a viable research strategy that enables a student to tackle the archives seriously and still complete within the required four years. But there is no doubt that such strategies will result in more specialized, more circumscribed and in many ways less ambitious research than used to be the case.

V

Ironically, perhaps, research in foreign archives itself is becoming easier in some ways. Most major archives now have online catalogues, and PhD students are increasingly taking a digital camera with them to photograph the files they need to use. This means they can gather a huge amount of material in a relatively short space of time, provided the archivist allows it, and take it back home to England to analyse in the comfort of their own study. The lengthy stays in cheap hotels in small provincial towns that were the lot of the PhD student studying French or German history when I embarked on my doctorate are no longer necessary. This carries with it a disadvantage, however: it is now possible to research a dissertation on the history of a foreign country while staying most of the time in the UK, which means that students are less likely to acquire a really thorough and intimate knowledge of the country, its culture and its people. In the end, too, as I tell my own PhD students when I see them packing their digital cameras for a quick raid on the archives in Leipzig or Berlin, they still have to read the documents they photograph, and they won't save a vast amount of time by doing this in Cambridge instead of *in situ*. In Geoffrey Hosking's view, indeed, the fact that it is easier to visit the Continent than ever before has meant that 'we have actually become *less* curious about the outside world in recent decades', so that 'foreign news occupies less space in newspapers, radio and television current affairs programmes' than it used to. Cheap air travel, he thinks, 'inclines us to treat foreign countries as consumer objects rather than as societies and cultures with their own internal life'.

The obstacles placed in the way of young historians who want to tackle broad and significant topics involving the use of foreign languages do not end nowadays with the PhD. For the last two decades, all Departments in British universities have been periodically subjected to a Research Assessment Exercise, in which a peer-review process grades their research output and the government adjusts research infrastructure funding accordingly. In future, this is likely to include a substantial element of 'bibliometric' assessment, in which the number of times the publications of members of any given Department are cited by other scholars is used as the basis for grading. All this means that from the very outset of their career, historians – like their counterparts in other fields – are under never-ending pressure to publish. To be sure, the Research Assessment Exercise concluded in 2008 did allow early-career historians to submit one or two publications instead of the four required of everyone else. But in general, the effect of the Research Assessment Exercise, as Geoffrey Hosking notes, has been that while 'scholars who established themselves before it came to have a decisive influence have been able to continue publishing works of broad outlook . . . for younger scholars, it is very difficult to make the breakthrough to a broader approach under the pressures

of unrelenting peer review, which tends to reinforce disciplinary boundaries and to impose rather rigid methodological
requirements'.

Sir Ian Kershaw points to another, perhaps subtler
deterrent, at least for those who want to work on recent or
contemporary history – always an attraction to graduate
research students, since they can exploit large quantities of
recently released and largely unread documentary sources,
unlike those who work on periods for which the archives have
already been combed by several generations of researchers.
'With the exception perhaps of 1989–91', he suspects, 'modern
European history has been rather less "dramatic" than the
era of the world wars and maybe less enticing to prospective
students.' In a similar way, the downgrading of the perceived
long-term significance of the French Revolution of 1789 by
François Furet and other historians who succeeded in demol-
ishing the Marxist interpretation that had held the field for
so many decades, coupled with the overwhelming flood of
publications that appeared on the bicentenary in 1989, seems
seriously to have lessened the attractiveness of the topic for
would-be researchers. Even the significance of the Third
Reich seems to have diminished as German historians and the
German public more generally move towards a normalization
of their own history.

Whatever the period you choose to work on, however,
the competition from Continental historians has grown steadily fiercer, as dictatorships, from Spain to East Germany,
Soviet Russia to Portugal, have crumbled, archives have
been opened up, and native historians have become free to
engage in unfettered scholarly research. Everywhere on the

Continent, as well as in the UK, universities have undergone a dramatic expansion, with the numbers of research students increasing, and more historians teaching and writing than ever before. Sir John Elliott remarks that, 'while I, and all my Cambridge research students working on Spanish or Latin American history, managed to complete their theses in three years, this was a pretty exacting process', not least because 'research in foreign archives involves a process of adaptation to a foreign environment and foreign sources which makes heavier demands than those faced by students working on the history of their own country, at least for the modern period'. However, he thinks, this is no longer really possible, and he concludes: 'The multiplication of research by Continental historians over the past few decades, and the vast increase in the secondary literature, now necessitate, in my opinion, the funding of an additional year for students engaged in research on foreign subjects.'

Christopher Duggan agrees that the tradition of British engagement with the history of Continental Europe is under threat:

> The key thing is for the British historical community,
> universities, the AHRC etc. to emphasise (in an era
> in which we are all being invited to focus on areas of
> competitive advantage) just how distinctive and strong
> this tradition is, and just how much the international
> standing of British historiography is linked to the
> receptiveness of countries such as Italy, German, Spain
> and Russia to the work of British historians. From this
> could flow a series of strategic initiatives, e.g. ensuring
> school curricula are not narrowly British, maintaining a

strong presence of non-British specialists in university History Departments, encouraging the acquisition of (and providing the means for learning) foreign languages by historians, offering extended (e.g. four-year) bursaries for those doing non-British history PhDs.

This view is echoed by many. David Moon, for instance, argues for modern languages to be made compulsory for all secondary school pupils up to the age of sixteen, as is the norm in most European countries apart from the UK. Language courses, he thinks, should also be made available as electives or subsidiaries at universities, as they are in Princeton and other leading American institutions. Whether this can be done depends, however, on wider cultural and political commitment in British society to the continuation of the long and influential tradition of writing about the European past.

VI

How serious is this commitment? Many historians are sceptical, even pessimistic. There has for some time, says David Welch, been a 'drip-drip of political pressure that has largely been antagonistic to the European ideal and has embraced, instead, new fads on citizenship etc.'. David Moon concurs: 'We are lagging behind American and German universities in producing high-quality European historians in sufficient numbers', he says, 'and I consider this incompatible with the UK's membership of the EU, and the wider outlook the UK needs to compete in the modern world.' But a sense of disengagement with Europe is not just evident in the political class, in government and in educational bureaucracies; some think it is also evident in the British historical profession itself. Robert Gildea, for example, sees the main threat to the British focus on European History coming 'from Global History rather than British History. Over the years', he says, 'I have noticed a shift of academic interest from French to German History, then to Russian History, now to Global, especially East Asian, History ... I don't necessarily think that it is either/or – the cult of Transnational History includes Europe as much as it excludes it, but Continental History is no longer the main alternative to British History.'

There may be some practical, financial considerations here – British and British Imperial History are thought by some university managers to be more likely to attract high-fee-paying overseas postgraduates, though there is not much evidence that this is really the case, and so preference is given to these fields when approving the advertising of teaching posts. As far as young researchers themselves are concerned, Alex Bamji suggests that 'perhaps some postgraduates who were once sufficiently adventurous to branch out from Britain to Europe are now drawn to wider World History'. Yet, at the same time, it is difficult to do Global History without a knowledge of European history and languages, whether it is Spanish and Portuguese for Latin America or French for much of Africa or Dutch for Indonesia or German for New Guinea, Namibia and Tanzania. The shadows left by European imperialism are long and deep. Sir John Elliott fears 'that the loss of empire has had the effect of limiting horizons' and of turning the British gaze inwards once more, after centuries of engagement with the wider world. While 'the global awareness of the new generation', he adds, may 'help to counter-balance this creeping parochialism, and sustain and revive the outward-looking tradition of British historians', there is of course no guarantee that any revival of the outward gaze will be directed specifically towards Europe.

For Christopher Duggan, whose views reflect his life-long preoccupation with Italian history, the wider problem lies in

> a cultural shift in the last 30 or so years that has made the dominant cultural paradigms for the young less 'European'. Elite culture till the 1970s was still (and there were obviously negative as well as positive aspects to this) heavily inflected with the Grand Tour/imperial ethos, with Classics and knowledge of European languages (and European literary classics) at their heart. That elite culture has been eroded by post-colonialism, the surge in non-literary paradigms, especially for the young, and, e.g., the 'democratization' of universities and institutions such as the BBC and civil service, the down-grading of language acquisition (the idea that everyone now speaks English), and the UK's uncomfortable relationship with the EU.

Robert Anderson points to a further cultural change, particularly in the educational system. When he went through school and university in the 1950s and 1960s, it was normal to stay on for a third year in the sixth form, with an Oxbridge scholarship exam taken in December, so that there was plenty of time to pursue one's own interests before going up to university. There was no pressure to take on vacation jobs. So he used the time to go to Florence and Rome, learn Italian, and spend time in the art galleries and museums pursuing an interest in art history. 'This sort of cultural visit to the Continent', he thinks, 'is no longer in fashion.' In his view the 'lack of pressure and freedom to develop new interests, at both school and university levels', encouraged students to take time out to learn languages and acquire a cultural hinterland: 'The pressure on students today makes this difficult, and it is reinforced by the obsession with assessment, and by the prevalent and in my view pernicious TQA-type pedagogy, with its emphasis on skills and outcomes rather than self-development.'

More generally, the British tradition of writing about the history of other countries is, says Norman Davies, 'a standing counterweight to the still stronger tradition of Anglocentric, insular, domestic and patriotic History. It has attracted a variety of dissidents, eccentrics, non-conformists and non-English, who', he says, 'have been less than impressed by "Our (inward-looking) Island Story".' Members of minorities within British culture may, he hypothesizes, have played a particular role here: 'Catholics and other religious misfits, people of Welsh, Irish or Scots origin, and immigrants, particularly Jewish immigrants. The minority perspective of all these groups may well have run counter to the narrowly Protestant, Anglican, English, patriotic and insular strain within the national culture.' Or to put it another way, as Sir John Elliott does, British historians' 'long engagement with foreign themes probably stems in part from the individualism, often bordering on eccentricity, that has characterized British society over the past three centuries, nourishing curiosity, and encouraging people to do their own thing'. 'The possession of overseas empire', continues Elliott, 'and our international dominance between the mid-18th and the mid-20th century to some extent mitigated our inherent tendencies to parochialism, and forced us to engage with societies other than our own.' Partly as a result of this, as Peter Jones observes, the British have, at least since the seventeenth century, 'been a pretty rootless people . . . a people who have traveled readily (at all social levels) and enquiringly'. More narrowly, perhaps, the tradition reflects, as Robert Mallett puts it, an 'intellectual curiosity . . . that is symptomatic of the British academic system at its best'.

David Abulafia thinks that while 'German, Italian and Spanish historians – not to mention any number of smaller nations – have been visibly grappling with issues concerning national identity' and thus put their work too often 'into the service of national myths', the 'softer tone of national feeling' in Britain, 'whether it is the result of being four "nations" somehow managing to coexist, or of the redirection of nationalism outwards into empire-building, or of an indefinable British dislike of political extremism of the sort espoused by so many nationalist groups', has impelled many British historians into working on other parts of the world; a perception supported, as we have seen, by Leif Jerram's observations on the differences between the range of university History courses available in Britain and, for example, those on offer in Spain.

Are these cultural traditions in decline? Some think so. British distrust of the European Union plays in the eyes of many a particularly baleful role that penetrates even the state education system. 'Our schooling', complains Robert Service, 'has a Kingsley Amis-style complacency and distaste for Abroad.' In debating with Tony Blair in Oxford a few years ago, he responded to the Prime Minister's claim that Britain's was the most 'European' of governments in regard to education by asking rhetorically: 'So why do Italians grow up knowing about Hume and Dickens while the young British think Dante is, if anything, a Derby winner?' 'The public encouragement of anti-European attitudes', says Rosamond McKitterick, 'does not help.' William Doyle finds that:

> The indifference of government to the decline of languages in schools is quite shocking. No other European country would tolerate it. It seems part and parcel of a general shrinking of horizons vis-à-vis Europe which really makes me despair. There seems to be a sort of knee-jerk hostility to anything emanating from the Continent which strikes me as quite irrational but amazingly widespread at every level of society. I'm sure it has deep historical roots but I'm amazed that thirty years of membership of the EU hasn't done more to convince the Brits of its obvious benefits and achievements.

Victoria Harris, who went to school and university in America in the 1990s and early 2000s before taking her doctorate at Cambridge, agrees. The British school curriculum, she thinks, is far narrower than her own schooling in the USA ('at a badly funded, inner-city state school') and involves far too little teaching about the world outside the UK. The lack of knowledge of other parts of the globe makes it more difficult for students 'to make the wide connections that people of their intelligence should' and impoverishes them intellectually as a result. And this reflects wider cultural developments. 'I am often taken aback', she confesses,

228

by how surprised Brits who don't study extra-British history, or who aren't academics themselves, are, when I tell them I study Germany. This is very different to the experience I've had in the United States . . . This country seems to be shrinking in on itself. As long as this mood persists, then I do think the study of other cultures, in history or otherwise, will be under threat. This wider cultural shift is partially responsible.

This shift, if that is what it is, can be observed in British schools too. Marisa Linton, author of *The Politics of Virtue in Enlightenment France*, published in 2001, notes that she meets 'fewer and fewer English academics working on my field. Even the most eminent historians of the French Revolution seem to have few or no doctoral students.' There is now little Continental History taught in the schools, she thinks, and what there is focuses overwhelmingly on twentieth-century Germany and Russia. Very few of the students she teaches at Kingston University have ever studied early modern Europe, and their almost total lack of language skills makes the subject seem more alien and off-putting still:

> When I teach the French Revolution as a third-year subject, I never give my students documents in French. But they still occasionally grumble that my teaching is too French. When I ask them what they mean by this, they say that they have difficulty with the names of people and places. I write the names in handouts, but the students do not know how to pronounce them, and so often fail to recognise them.

Such ignorance 'reflects a narrowing of English society and culture', she thinks: 'We are appreciably poorer for assuming that other countries should learn our language, but that we should not learn their language or culture.'

Yet there are some who see things less blackly. Robert Service still considers that 'we are much more tolerant of national and cultural idiosyncrasies in the UK than is true of several other European countries.' Perhaps this is another way of saying that Britain is more of a multicultural society than most. 'The British schooling system', observes Peter Jones, 'is defiantly multicultural, and I think that no government will succeed in forcing upon kids the "our island story" version of history. My wife', he adds, 'is Head of Sixth in a girls' grammar school in multicultural Birmingham, and the most popular history module is Russia in the nineteenth and twentieth centuries.' For school students belonging to ethnic minorities, studying Russian or French or German history may be less encumbered with collective memories and family histories than studying the history of the British Empire or the areas that used to belong to it. Multiculturalism doesn't necessarily involve an interest in the culture of Europe; rather, indeed, it brings with it an interest in the culture of other parts of the world. Nevertheless, Britain is part of Europe, and, next to British History, publications, broadcasts and at least university teaching on European history will remain for the foreseeable future a significant part of the national culture, as it has been at least since the end of the Second World War. Britain is and will remain, a multicultural society in which it makes no sense to narrow down History teaching to a patriotic recitation of 'Our Island Story', as some politicians have occasionally advocated. Traditional British values of tolerance, acceptance of immigrants and minorities, curiosity about other cultures, sympathy for the underdog in past and present, at home and abroad, remain vitally important and need to be cherished. European History has been an important part of this cosmopolitan national identity.

Cosmopolitanism, of course, cuts many different ways. British historians who write on the European Continent do not simply apply to their subjects the empirical and literary traditions in which they have been trained; they have also been heavily influenced by the theories and methods deployed by historians in the countries they study, including, notably, for example, the *Annales* school in France, the Bielefeld and Fischer schools in Germany, and the Gramscian interpretation of the *risorgimento* in Italy. More generally, Continental thought has at many different times affected the way historians approach the British as well as the Continental past, from German historical method in the nineteenth century to the theories and approaches of Marx, Weber, Gramsci or Foucault in the twentieth. German, Italian and other historians now teaching European History in British universities bring with them many such theories and methods, as well as the experience of debates, arguments and controversies within their own national historiographical traditions, just as the German exiles did in the 1940s and 1950s, and teaching and research are all the richer for it. Intercultural and transnational history would probably barely exist in British universities – given the reluctance of British historians to engage in comparisons and their general lack of the multilingual capacities that would enable them to do so – but for the influx of young History teachers and researchers from the Continent.

231

Both groups, the older British historians and the younger German or Italian historians now teaching in British universities, are cultural mediators between different countries, though in rather different ways; both, in the end, are hybrids. On the Continent, the willingness of Italian, German and Spanish historians, students and the general reading public to enter into a dialogue with British (and American) historians about the history of their own country has few parallels in the United Kingdom, and bespeaks a kind of cosmopolitanism of its own. For British historians, indeed, distance from Europe has always been the essential precondition for studying it, and that remains the case today, for all Richard Cobb's romantic vision of a 'second identity'. British historians of Europe are thus undeniably cosmopolitan, but they are islanders too, and the Channel and the North Sea continue to be essential factors in conditioning their view. The fact that 'British' and 'European' History remain essentially separate in UK universities, a division that has no parallel in Continental countries, has its own rationale and speaks volumes about the distance that still separates the islanders from the inhabitants of the Continent.

If European History is to continue to be an important part of British multicultural national identity, then clearly the British educational system at all levels needs to take the teaching of European languages more seriously than it has been doing of late. The reinstatement of the requirement to learn a foreign language to GCSE-level would be a vital first step. This would free up universities to put on top-up courses as part of a wider commitment to the use of languages in the appropriate contexts, which of course include History. In the History

Faculty at Cambridge, for instance, we have devised two new undergraduate courses involving a combination of documents in either French or German with advanced language teaching provided by specialists. This kind of model could be expanded to cover other languages too. Joint History–Language degrees are also vital. Further up the educational ladder, the AHRC and ESRC seriously need to consider additional funding for graduate students who choose to do their research on a topic involving the use of a foreign language and the study of a foreign culture. These considerations apply, of course, just as much to Global History as they do to European; but Global History is vital in a globalized age, and needs languages just as much as European History does. The British tradition of writing broad, accessible scholarly works on European History does not necessarily depend, I have argued, on European History being taught by British-born historians, but encouraging more British-born and British-educated historians to take it up will help in its defence.

Where does this leave British History? Traditionally, as Robert Anderson remarks, it included a 'strong dose of foreign policy. Philip II and Louis XIV, the French Revolution and Napoleon, the Crimea and the Congress of Berlin, Versailles and appeasement, all came into "British" history in this way, in schools as well.' Paradoxically, perhaps, the emergence first of social and economic and then of cultural History and the relative downgrading of political and diplomatic History led to a perceptible narrowing of focus onto purely British aspects of the past. British history in the early twenty-first century is thus more 'British' than it was half a century ago. In this sense, the growth of European and Global

History has been compensatory rather than additional. Yet it is in many ways rather artificial to oppose the study of British History to the study of European. In a rapidly globalizing world, we are more conscious than ever of the links that bind our country to others, and in the early twenty-first century it is clear that British historians are increasingly viewing the history of their own country in a series of wider contexts – European, Imperial, global. Comparative, transnational and intercultural History are growing at the expense of a narrower focus on the history of a single country, whether it be Britain, France, Germany, Italy or Russia. It remains vitally important to study the history of our own country at every level, from primary school to PhD; it is an essential part of our national identity. But our national identity coexists, as in fact it has always done, with many other kinds of identity too, local, regional, immigrant, European, 'Western' – and studying these kinds of history is important too. Europe is an essential part of this wider picture. However it is taught, and whoever teaches it, as Lucy Riall concludes, 'Europe continues to inspire and fascinate the British imagination', and if British-based European historians continue to produce interesting work, then 'students will continue to want to study Europe', and the reading, viewing and thinking public in Britain will continue to want to learn about its past.

There is only one existing treatment of this topic, coincidentally by Robert Evans, Regius Professor of History at Oxford: 'The Creighton Century: British Historians and Europe, 1907–2007', delivered as the centenary Creighton Lecture in the University of London in 2007 and forthcoming in *Historical Research*. A typically elegant and penetrating account, it focuses above all on previous Creighton Lectures that have dealt with topics in Continental European History. As Evans remarks, existing surveys of British historical scholarship generally neglect the European dimension. The most entertaining is undoubtedly John Kenyon, *The History Men* (Pittsburgh, 1984, 2nd edn, London, 1991), the most critical Christopher Parker, *The English Historical Tradition since 1850* (Edinburgh, 1990), the most urbane Michael Bentley, *Modernizing England's Past: English Historiography in the Age of Modernism, 1870–1970* (Cambridge, 2003). Ranging somewhat further afield, but with the same absence of treatment of British historians of Europe, is Peter Burke (ed.), *History and Historians in the Twentieth Century* (Oxford, 2002). Stefan Berger, Mark Donovan and Kevin Passmore (eds.), *Writing National Histories: Western Europe since 1800* (London, 1999), focuses on domestic historical writing in a number of European countries.

Amongst general histories of History, John Burrow, *A History of Histories: Epics, Chronicles, Romances and Inquiries*

from Herodotus and Thucydides to the Twentieth Century
(London, 2007), is the most readable. Burrow notes that
Britain 'has been remarkable for the range of its attention
to the histories of other countries . . . No historical imperative', he adds, 'seems to have dictated that English historians
should have become leading authorities, even in those countries themselves, on the histories of Spain, Italy, Poland and
Sweden, but such has been the case.' However, he expends so
much space and energy on covering ancient, medieval and
early modern historians in the book that he runs out of breath,
as it were, by the time he gets to the twentieth century, and
does not attempt an explanation of the phenomenon he so
correctly identifies.

    Comparative studies are rare, but Georg G. Iggers,
New Directions in Historiography (Hanover, NH, 1984) and
Historiography in the Twentieth Century (Hanover, NH,
1997), are intelligent analyses, in the UK context focusing
perhaps excessively on the British Marxist historians, who
are also dealt with in Harvey J. Kaye, *The British Marxist
Historians* (Cambridge, 1984). Neither of them has very much
to say about the British historical interest in Europe, however.
Benedikt Stuchtey and Peter Wende (eds.), *British and
German Historiography, 1750–1950: Traditions, Perceptions,
and Transfers* (Oxford, 2000), is a lively collection of essays,
bringing out with particular clarity the methodological impact
of the German historians on British historical practice.

    Edward Gibbon has been the subject of a variety of
critical and biographical studies, of which Roy Porter, *Gibbon:
Making History* (2nd edn, London, 1995), is perhaps the best
short introduction. Gibbon's own *The History of the Decline*

and Fall of the Roman Empire is available in a variety of editions, both full and abridged, as is his *Autobiography*; there is an oft-reprinted edition in the Oxford World's Classics series. There is a useful monograph by Hedva Ben-Israel Kidron, *English Historians on the French Revolution* (Cambridge, 2002), which puts the work of Smyth, Allison and their successors in context and takes the story up to the end of the nineteenth century. Thomas Carlyle's *The French Revolution* has often been reprinted, his *Frederick the Great* seldom. Rosemary Ashton, *Thomas and Jane Carlyle: Portrait of a Marriage* (London, 2003), is the most rounded portrait of the man, his life and his works.

Good biographies of classic British historians who wrote on Europe include Deborah Wormell, *Sir John Seeley and the Uses of History* (Cambridge, 1979); Roland Hill, *Lord Acton* (London, 2000); and David Cannadine, *G. M. Trevelyan: A Life in History* (London, 1998). Acton's *Lectures on Modern History* were reprinted in a Fontana paperback in 1960 with an introduction by Hugh Trevor-Roper, who saw him as one of the great Victorian misfits, a cosmopolitan in an age of nationalism, an aristocratic pessimist in an era of bourgeois optimism. *The Cambridge Modern History*, still available in most older libraries, is a useful source for British writings on European history in the early part of the twentieth century. Trevelyan's *Garibaldi's Defence of the Roman Republic* (London, 1907), *Garibaldi and the Thousand* (London, 1909) and *Garibaldi and the Making of Italy* (London, 1911) have similarly been reprinted and are still worth reading. The broader background to Trevelyan's enthusiasm is filled in by John Pemble, *The Mediterranean Passion:*

Victorians and Edwardians in the South (Oxford, 1987). The manifestos of the great historical journals founded in the late nineteenth century are usefully reprinted in Fritz Stern (ed.), *The Varieties of History: From Voltaire to the Present* (Cleveland, OH, 1956).

British engagement with Central and Eastern Europe in the early part of the twentieth century is surveyed in Hugh and Christopher Seton-Watson, *The Making of a New Europe: R. W. Seton-Watson and the Last Years of Austria-Hungary* (London, 1981); Robert Seton-Watson's books were mostly contemporary political studies, and if he wrote history, it was the history of British foreign policy, signalling the link between his concerns and the making of British diplomacy. *Disraeli, Gladstone and the Eastern Question: A Study in Diplomacy and Party Politics* (London, 1935) is probably his best-known historical work. His son Hugh Seton-Watson's most notable historical work is *The Decline of Imperial Russia* (London, 1952); his later volume on Russia in the Oxford History of Modern Europe basically says the same things at vastly greater length. Christopher Seton-Watson's major work was *Italy from Liberalism to Fascism, 1870–1925* (London, 1967), whose gestation he dates to his participation in 'the final fifteen months of the Italian campaign' as he fought his way up the peninsula 'from Cassino to Bologna'. Sir Bernard Pares's fascinating but not always reliable autobiography, *My Russian Memoirs* (London, 1935), is corrected by the account by his son, Richard Pares, prefaced to the 1949 reprint of Bernard Pares, *A History of Russia* (London, 1926).

The impact of the First World War on historians in Britain can be gleaned from the relevant passages of Stuart

Wallace, *War and the Image of Germany: British Academics, 1914–1918* (Edinburgh, 1988). During the interwar years, the involvement of diplomatic historians in the making of foreign policy has spawned a number of scholarly studies. John D. Fair, *Harold Temperley: A Scholar and Romantic in the Public Realm, 1879–1939* (Newark, DE, 1992), is a solid biography. Frank Eyck, *G. P. Gooch: A Study in History and Politics* (London, 1982), is full of detail but less than easy to read. P. A. Reynolds and E. J. Hughes, *The Historian as Diplomat: Charles Kingsley Webster and the United Nations, 1939–1946* (London, 1976), underlines the mixture of government service and academic life characteristic of interwar diplomatic historians. Sir John (J. A. R.) Marriott, *Memories of Four Score Years. The Autobiography of Sir John Marriott* (London, 1946), is a charming account that underlines the dual role of so many historians of Europe during this era. For the general context, see Keith M. Wilson (ed.), *Forging the Collective Memory: Government and International Historians through Two World Wars* (Providence, RI, 1996).

A. J. P. Taylor, *A Personal History* (London, 1983), is typically contrarian, and needs to be corrected and supplemented by the detailed life by Chris Wrigley, *A. J. P. Taylor: Radical Historian of Europe* (London, 2006); the readable study by Adam Sisman, *A. J. P. Taylor: A Biography* (London, 1994); and the well-informed account by one of Taylor's PhD students, Kathleen Burk, *Troublemaker: The Life and History of A. J. P. Taylor* (London, 2000). Jonathan Haslam, *The Vices of Integrity: E. H. Carr, 1892–1982* (London, 1999), by one of Carr's PhD students, is psychologically acute and intellectually penetrating. Stefan Collini, *Absent Minds: Intellectuals in Britain* (Oxford, 2006), and the same author's *Common Reading; Historians, Critics, Publics* (Oxford, 2008) provide acute critical accounts of Taylor, Carr and others.

Peter Alter (ed.), *Out of the Third Reich: Refugee Historians in Post-War Britain* (London, 1998), contains autobiographical essays by Francis Carsten, John Grenville, Peter Hennock, Helli Koenigsberger, Werner Mosse, Sidney Pollard, Peter Pulzer, Walter Ullmann and other exiles. For the story on the other side of the Atlantic, see Hartmut Lehmann and James J. Sheehan (eds.), *An Interrupted Past: German-Speaking Refugee Historians in the United States after 1933* (Washington, DC, 2002). An exile of an earlier generation, Sir Lewis Namier, made his reputation with his studies of eighteenth-century British history, analysed in Linda Colley, *Lewis Namier* (London, 1989), though he also wrote a good deal about nineteenth- and twentieth-century Europe; Amy Ng, *Nationalism and Political Liberty: Redlich, Namier and the Crisis of Empire* (Oxford, 2004), deals with his early career.

On the wartime historians, William Palmer, *Engagement with the Past: The Lives and Works of the World War II Generation of Historians* (Lexington, KY, 2001), tries to find common features in British and American historians who became involved in the war, but tackles the subject on too narrow a front really to succeed, despite having some interesting things to say about Cobb, Trevor-Roper and others along the way. A biography of Hugh Trevor-Roper by Adam Sisman will shortly appear, but for the moment the best biographical information about this generation of British historians can be found in the *Proceedings of the British Academy*, divided in recent years into two volumes containing, respectively, lectures and 'Memoirs' or obituaries; the latter are often lengthy and detailed and the best of them can sometimes be very revealing. More basic data can be retrieved from the *Oxford Dictionary of National Biography*. Among autobiographies, Michael Howard, *Captain Professor: A Life in War and Peace* (London, 2006), is an entertaining memoir, and Eric Hobsbawm, *Interesting Times: A Twentieth-Century Life* (London, 2002), a fascinating account of History on the left.

In the case of Richard Cobb, it is difficult to disentangle History from biography, but the best starting-point for his life and ideas is probably *A Second Identity: Essays on France and French History* (Oxford, 1969); his last book, *The End of the Line* (London, 1997), has further autobiographical essays. Gwynne Lewis and Colin Lucas (eds.), *Beyond the Terror: Essays in French Regional and Social History, 1794–1815* (Cambridge, 1983), the *Festschrift* for Cobb, presents the work of many of his pupils. As far as contemporary British historians are concerned, Daniel Snowman, *Historians* (London, 2007), contains subtle and mostly sympathetic critical accounts and biographies, partly based on interviews with a variety of historians, including a number of Britons who have written extensively on the European past, such as Eric Hobsbawm, Peter Burke, Theodore Zeldin, Geoffrey Hosking, Ian Kershaw, Orlando Figes, Niall Ferguson and Norman Davies.

To list even a brief sample of British historians' writings on Europe here would take up far too much space; the best way forward for anyone unfamiliar with them is simply to follow up the references in the text through internet, library or booksellers' catalogues or to browse the European History shelves in any good bookshop. There are many highly readable works on general European, Dutch, French, German, Italian, Russian, Spanish and other history available, written by British historians, as I hope this book has made clear.

INDEX

Indonesia 224
Institute of Historical Research 20
institutes 10–11, 20–1, 157
Inter Nationes 22
Israel, Jonathan 4, 7
Italy
British fascination with 93,
96–100, 180–1, 187, 225–6
British historians of 3, 17, 92–101,
122, 139
in Italian universities 36
reception in Italy 32–6, 51–2
British School in Rome 20
colonialism 98
comparative history 13
domestic history 18, 19, 20
early modern period 5
Fascist period 20, 32, 33–4, 99, 180
foreign history 12, 13, 14, 15, 16, 18,
19
historical tradition 52
Italian historians in Britain 204,
206–7, 232
Italian historians of Britain 6, 19
languages 200
Middle Ages 82
Napoleon and 89
popularity with foreign historians
17, 19
Risorgimento 93, 94–9, 231
school curricula 228
subsidized translations 22
Trevelyan on 96–100
unification 33, 98, 99, 108, 181
witchcraft 52

Jackson, Gabriel 53
Jacobsen, Arne 183
Jamaica 184
James II 94

Jena, Battle of (1806) 80
Jerram, Leif 7–8, 173, 175–6, 183,
196, 227
Johns, Captain William Earl
(W. E.) 165
Joll, James 139, 179
Jones, Colin 153
Jones, Peter 39, 166, 175, 206–7,
227, 230
journals 4, 91–2
Juan Carlos, King 44

Kant, Immanuel 7
Kantorowicz, Ernst 127
Kaye, Harvey J. 236
Keen, Maurice 190
Kenyon, John 1–2, 3, 235
Kershaw, Sir Ian 3, 5, 24, 25, 26, 54,
56, 137–9, 168, 177, 202, 215–16,
221, 241
Kidron, Hedva Ben-Israel 237
Kindertransport 129
Kingsley, Charles 77–9
Kipling, Rudyard 165
Kirby, David 4
Kirk, Tim 176–7, 204
Koenigsberger, Helli (H. G.) 129,
240
Kossuth, Lajos 94
Kümin, Beat 206

languages
acquisition by immersion 195–6
archives and 218–22
bilingualism 195
British students' ignorance of 9,
229
comparative history and 13–14
compulsory learning 223, 232
cultural changes 223–34

255